Dear Traders, THERE IS MAGIC IN RSI

Dear Traders, THERE IS MAGIC IN RSI

RSI Tells the Secrets
Are You Listening?

SUDHIR DIXIT

AMARYLLIS

AMARYLLIS

An imprint of Manjul Publishing House Pvt. Ltd.
• C-16, Sector 3, Noida, Uttar Pradesh 201301, India
Website: www.manjulindia.com
Registered Office:
• 2nd Floor, Usha Preet Complex,
42, Malviya Nagar, Bhopal 462 003 - India
Distribution Centres
Ahmedabad, Bengaluru, Chennai, Hyderabad,
Kochi, Kolkata, Mumbai, Noida, Pune

Dear Traders, There is Magic in RSI by Sudhir Dixit

This edition first published in India in 2025
Second impression 2026

ISBN 978-93-7317-867-7

Printed and bound in India by Repro India Ltd.

Contents

	Disclaimer	7
	Acknowledgements	9
	Who Is a Trader?	13
	Introduction: Why Is the RSI So Magical?	15
1	The Hidden Challenges of RSI Trading	19
2	The Birth and Growth of the RSI	27
3	The Real Secret of the RSI Is in Its Calculation Method	33
4	The Top 10 Signals of the RSI	50
5	Divergences: Bullish and Bearish	69
6	Reversals: Positive and Negative	86
7	Limitations of the RSI	98
8	Which Timeframe Is Best?	101
9	20 Popular RSI Trading Strategies	114

10 Busting the Myth: Can the RSI Remain Oversold/Overbought for Several Months? 125

11 Additional Tips 128

Feedback 132

Disclaimer

The author is not an investment advisor and the information being given in this book is for study purposes only. Information is being presented without consideration of the investment objectives, risk tolerance or financial circumstances of any specific investor. You are responsible for your own investment decisions. We urge our readers to seek professional advice before acting on the basis of any information contained in this book.

Acknowledgements

Nobody is an island; we all need mastermind groups to help us grow and hone our skillsets.

I wish to thank all the members of my Facebook groups, who are burning the midnight oil to take their learning to the next level.

It is said that RSI moves precede price moves; likewise, learning precedes earning in the stock market.

In particular, I wish to thank The Trader's Code group, the Fundotechno Investors group, the Amibroker AFL Collection, and their members and admins: Abhishek Ninaniya, Dinesh Bohra & Syam Palakkal, and Rajen Vyas. I feel privileged to be a part of these groups, as I have learnt a lot there. And the learning process is still ongoing.

I am thankful to Spider Software India and Investing.com for helping me prepare the charts used in the book.

And I would especially like to extend my gratitude to Anish Thomas for providing me Andrew Cardwell's tapes on the RSI. Thank you, Anish! Your help is all the more appreciated, as you helped without asking.

"Even though we do not suggest using only one indicator, if one had to, the 2-period RSI would be the indicator."

— Larry Connors, Founder,
Connors Research

Who Is a Trader?

For the purposes of this book, a trader is someone who wants high short-term performance on the basis of technical analysis, whereas an investor is someone who makes long-term investments on the basis of fundamental analysis.

Most technical analysts are traders by default, though some analysts may be investors due to their usage of a mix of fundamental and technical analysis.

INTRODUCTION

Why Is the RSI So Magical?

"I haven't found anything in over thirty years of work that can hold a candle to what RSI can do."

— Andrew Cardwell

All of us have some kind of natural affinity with a particular indicator, which seems to tell us something more than it tells other people. There's instant chemistry and a natural bond between us and the indicator—we become fast friends! Different indicators appeal to different people, so the first thing we should do is select our favourite indicator. For me, it is the RSI; for you, it may be the MACD, CCI, money flow index, WMA, or any other indicator. Our task is to recognise our favourite indicator and to use it more often, as it is more likely to increase our odds of success.

Let me tell you one thing in advance: it is by coincidence that you are reading this book, because I wrote it for myself! I wanted to gather and condense all the important information, insights, learnings, and experiences I had collected concerning the RSI, which lay scattered here and there, in one place... and publishing a book was just the right carrot to motivate me!

I can guarantee you that after reading this book, you will be more able to understand and appreciate the magical signals of the RSI. And maybe the magic of the RSI will rub off on you, and you will start loving it the same way that I do!

> *"The Relative Strength Index (RSI) is perhaps the most popular of all technical oscillators, in that it provides an easy-to interpret indication of possible market turning points and trend strength."*
>
> **— Matthew Clements,**
> **editor of *The Technical Analyst* magazine**

Let me honestly admit that before writing this book, I thought I knew a lot about the RSI, but the research process for the book has humbled me. During my research, I went through several books, dozens of blogs/articles, and Andrew Cardwell's tapes. Then I realised that there was so much that I didn't know! And by the same logic, there may be much that I still don't know. However, I have honestly tried to get as much in-depth knowledge about the RSI as I could. I don't claim to know everything about the RSI, but what I know is worth telling.

To me, the RSI is a fascinating and dynamic indicator. Others may consider it solely a momentum oscillator, which works more effectively in a range-bound market, but trust me, it can give you significant signals even in trending markets. If you don't believe me, at least believe Andrew Cardwell, who said, "I haven't found anything in over thirty years of work that can hold a candle to what RSI can do."

Most other indicators, like moving averages, are lagging indicators, as they lack predictive power. On the other hand, the RSI is a **leading indicator** that can give significant clues about future prices—if we have the ability to decode them.

I call the RSI magical because it can predict prices and tell us where to get in and where to get out.

In a nutshell, these are some of the most important things the RSI can do for us:

- The RSI can tell us whether the price is likely to go up or down (momentum).
- The RSI can warn us through divergences, when a trend is beginning to change (slowdown of momentum).
- The RSI can give us trend continuation signals through positive and negative reversals (Andrew Cardwell's brainchildren).
- The RSI can even help us set price objectives for negative and positive reversals (again Andrew Cardwell's discovery).
- The RSI can pretty accurately tell us in advance whether a breakout is going to happen in a channel or a pattern (because it is a leading indicator).
- The RSI can tell us when to buy and when to sell (this was the whole purpose for which Wilder invented it).

And if you take the trouble of using a screener on RSI signals, the RSI can even give you a list of good buying options too.

Not a bad idea!

If an indicator can tell us all that, don't you think we should learn more about it?

Remember, for succeeding in the stock market, we need to know just three things:

1. **What to buy?**
2. **When to buy?**
3. **When to sell?**

The RSI can tell us all these three things, and more!

Read on for further details.

CHAPTER 1

The Hidden Challenges of RSI Trading

"The RSI indicator is a cruel mistress! She lures us in with promises of easy money and trading success, only to drain your trading account balance in a run of terrible stoploss strikes, even though the indicator said BUY! The RSI indicator is usually the go to oscillator for the novice trader when deciding to enter that first trade. There is a simple, valid reason for this: The RSI indicator is simple to read and understand."

— From a HumbleTraders.com article

Trading on the basis of the RSI looks easy at first sight. But my goodness, is it complicated at its core! The above quote sums up the situation pretty accurately.

There are certain challenges, due to which the RSI may perhaps be the most complex indicator in the whole stock market universe. Most traders don't know about these challenges or don't bother about them and then wonder why the RSI doesn't work for them.

This book will tell you about these hidden challenges, which are like roadblocks in serious RSI-based trading.

You see, most of us use indicators without knowing their secrets.

For example, when I started learning technical analysis, I didn't know how the RSI is calculated, why it gives divergences, or why it is called a leading indicator.

More importantly, it never occurred to me that learning these things was important, as such.

For me, the RSI was just another indicator like the MACD or the Ultimate Oscillator. So I kept on using them with the help of Investopedia and other such online platforms.

Of course, back then, I didn't know about positive and negative reversals. In fact, all my (little) knowledge about the RSI could have fit onto the back of a postage stamp! But was I humble? No way!

Perhaps you are in the same boat. You see, we discover one or two tricks, by reading or by chance, and consider ourselves masters of the RSI or any other oscillator. We don't take the trouble of digging deep into one indicator, but keep on switching indicators in search of the magical indicator.

Just remember that you can't succeed in digging a well by digging 100 different shallow holes. If you wish to dig a well, keep on digging in the same spot. And if you are going to dig deep anywhere in the stock market, let that place be the RSI. If we dig deep, perhaps we may strike gold!

I focus only on the RSI, and I have never switched my focus, so you can rest assured that I have dug somewhat deeper than normal (though due to my other professional preoccupations, I am unable to devote much time to the stock market). For another thing, I have never traded positive or negative reversals, so I don't have any practical knowledge about them. I have traded RSI divergences a lot and I can vouch for their effectiveness. Lastly, I have never shorted, so this book is written with a buyer's bias.

Now I am going to tell you the pitfalls or challenges which an RSI trader usually faces, about which he may be blissfully unaware.

Lack of RSI Studies in the Indian Context

You see, acquiring in-depth knowledge about the RSI or any other indicator is pretty difficult. For this, we need the help of good books, a lot of exclusive practice, and a thorough discussion of the indicator's successes or failures in the Indian context. We trade in the Indian stock market with the rules which were written for U.S. markets.

Unfortunately, most Indian websites and Indian books contain copied-and-pasted material from foreign websites and books. Nobody has seriously bothered to check whether foreign RSI techniques work in the Indian context or not (you will see in this book that some of them don't work at all times, or at all). We seriously lack native study material. What works in the American market may not necessarily work in the Indian market.

Of course, there are several Indian blogs, trading forums, and stock market Facebook pages where you can occasionally find discussions about technical indicators, but unfortunately, there is a lack of serious discussion about technical indicators and their mysteries.

Lack of Books on the RSI

Even in the U.S., not many books are exclusively devoted to the RSI. In most books, you will only find a 10-page chapter on the RSI that more or less repeats the same information you can find in other books.

Additionally, whatever books have been written have their own hidden agendas behind them. They have been used to promote the authors' own trading systems, indicators, or investment firms. For example, Paul Dean has written some useful booklets on the RSI, but they have been largely written to promote his RSI Paint Indicator.

John Hayden has written a good book on the RSI, but he promotes a charting program for professional traders, with an eye to sell a particular RSI tool.

Andrew Cardwell has, of course, done a lot to popularise the RSI, but he was also intent on selling his audio programs; he has since un-published his book, as the audio programs proved more lucrative.

So, you see, the RSI is the neglected child of the stock market universe. And those who have adopted it have their own axe to grind.

The Challenge of the Timeframe

Any discussion on the RSI will be at cross-purposes unless you clearly spell out your timeframe. Most problems occur and most signals fail just because we apply the RSI strategy for one timeframe to another timeframe, where it is out of place. No wonder it then fails to give the intended results!

You see, what works in a daily chart may not work in a weekly chart, and vice versa. Perhaps this is why we see a lot of conflicting opinions regarding the RSI. Those who trade on 1-minute charts are laying down rules on their blogs, and daily chart investors are left wondering why those rules are not working for them.

Mind the timeframe of the chart!

Wilder invented the RSI for daily charts! Andrew Cardwell preferred weekly charts! No wonder their techniques are so diametrically different.

Always remember that RSI tricks which work in one timeframe may or may not work in another timeframe.

In this book, we mainly discuss the RSI in terms of daily timeframes, though at certain places, weekly or minute charts have also been given. (We will discuss timeframes at length in a later chapter!)

The Challenge of the RSI Period

To add to the confusion, the RSI can be set to different periods, which may give very different results.

Wilder had set a period of 14 days for his daily chart.

But in order to get more signals, day traders tamper with this setting and use a shorter period, like 9 periods or 3 periods. Long-term investors use settings for a longer period, like 21 periods or so. So neither their experiences nor their findings will be much useful for conventional investors unless they trade by modifying the RSI periods.

Target Markets Are Different

You see, there are several markets in the world. Whatever has been written for forex traders (like Paul Dean's books) may not be useful for a stock market trader, because movements in a forex market are on a smaller level, so a gain or loss of 1 dollar in price is seen as a heavy gain or loss. Likewise, RSI strategies of commodity traders, bond traders, and the like may not succeed in stock markets. When target markets are different, successful strategies are apt to be different as well. What succeeds in one market may not necessarily succeed in another.

This book is specifically written for the Indian context. It is largely written for short-term traders (whose timeframe is less than a year), though most of the findings can be applied by day traders and long-term investors as well.

RSI Readings Differ on Different Software Tools/Websites

Of course, there are several stock market blogs and Facebook groups in which traders post their findings on the RSI, but I found, to my dismay, that these are not always reliable. The simple reason is that due to smoothening or data length mismatches, RSI readings are different on different websites or charting software tools. So when you are talking about a bearish divergence on the RSI, it may turn out that in reality, there was no bearish divergence, and you mistakenly thought so due to the wrong RSI reading from your software.

Most people love free software tools. But their RSI readings do not match. This is why Chartink screeners have limited scope for RSI-specific trading strategies, as its RSI readings are found to be inconsistent. Of course, we can develop our own successful trading system based on wrong readings through trial and error, but conventional strategies may not work there.

I would like to give an example of this:

The ChartNexus reading of the RSI for April 30, 2020 for Nifty (daily) is above 70, whereas in Traders Cockpit, it is 59.59 in.

So if you trade on the signal from ChartNexus, you are going to trade wrong. However, if you tweak the settings and use the RSI smoothed indicator, you come close.

Another example of RSI readings in a 1-hour chart at close for April 30, 2020:

- **Chartink reading:** 77.59.
- **Investing.com reading:** 76.53.
- **Traders Cockpit reading:** 75.51.

They are different! They do not match! Though the difference doesn't look big, at critical junctures (like overbought/oversold levels), such a difference can matter a lot.

To avoid any such confusion, for the purposes of this book, I have relied on the RSI readings of Investing.com and Spider Software.

Important Tip

RSI readings are different on different software tools, so be cautious. Whenever you make a trade on the basis of RSI readings, make sure that you are trading based on the correct readings, as given by Investing.com.

Terminology Clutter

In the RSI world, there is so much confusion regarding price/RSI divergence due to its many variations—most of them quite unnecessary and repetitive. There is bullish RSI divergence, bearish RSI divergence, positive RSI divergence, negative RSI divergence, positive reversal, negative reversal, regular RSI divergence, classical RSI divergence, hidden bullish divergence, hidden bearish divergence, etc. It looks like every expert came in and gave a new name to different RSI patterns.

In this book, we will discuss at length four price/RSI divergence patterns: bullish divergence and bearish divergence (both by Wilder), and positive reversal and negative reversal (both by Cardwell). All the terms mentioned above are covered in these four RSI signals.

Hmm!

Now that we've got a fair idea of the challenges involved with actually putting the RSI into practice, we should move on to the beginning, where this whole RSI story started. Let us see how the RSI was invented, and for what purpose.

CHAPTER 2

The Birth and Growth of the RSI

"RSI measures momentum—momentum is perhaps the most important factor in trading. If you understand momentum, you are 90% of the way home."

— Paul Dean

The Relative Strength Index, or RSI, was invented by J. Welles Wilder. He described it in his 1978 book, *New Concepts in Technical Trading Systems.*

Strangely enough, he describes the RSI in only 8 pages, and for the rest of the book, he discusses and describes other tools and indicators at greater length.

This is interesting! Even the creator didn't fully appreciate the significance of the RSI! Even Wilder didn't know that one day, the RSI would become one of the topmost and most popular indicators in the stock market universe. If he had known that, he would have devoted the whole book to the RSI alone.

What Is the RSI?

Simply speaking, the RSI is a momentum oscillator, measured on a scale from 0 to 100. On this scale, high and low levels are marked at 70 and 30, which respectively show overbought and oversold levels.

The default period for the RSI in a daily chart is 14 days. Just see the chart below to get an idea:

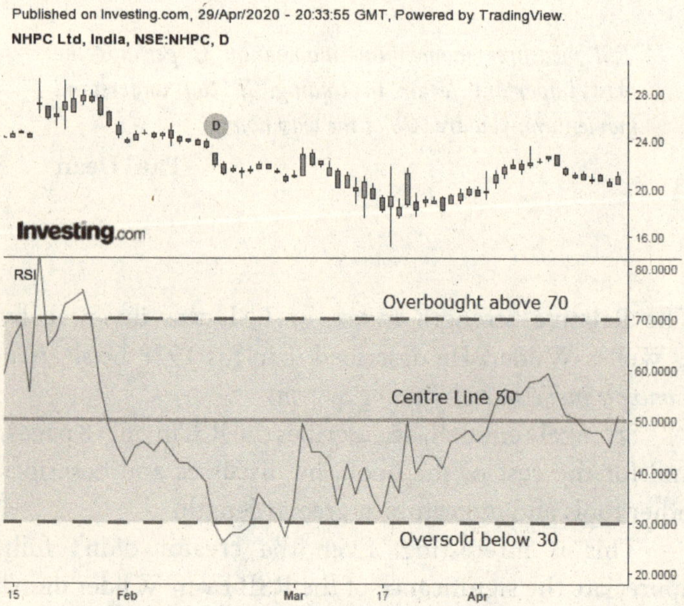

The Lines and Zones on the RSI Panel

For the sake of clarity, let us analyse the above NHPC chart. You will find price action on the top panel, while the RSI is on the bottom panel.

- The shaded area from 30 to 70 shows the normal range of the RSI, where it is neither overbought nor oversold.
- The RSI is considered oversold below 30 and overbought above 70.
- There is a centreline at level 50, which is the exact centre of the RSI scale (from 0–100) as well as its normal range (from 30–70).

Now we will observe the RSI movements on its panel. In this chart, the RSI line crosses above 70 (overbought level). Then it slides down to 30 (oversold level) and penetrates it. Then it pushes up and touches the centreline, which you can see at level 50. And then it breaks the centreline.

You will need to remember all of this, as it will be handy when we discuss RSI signals, patterns, and strategies.

Why Was the RSI Invented?

J. Welles Wilder was an American mechanical engineer turned technical analyst, best known for his work in technical analysis.

Wilder is the father of several technical indicators that are now considered to be core indicators in technical analysis software tools. These include the *Average True Range*, the *Relative Strength Index* (RSI), the *Average Directional Index*, and the *Parabolic SAR*.

Wilder was a trader and technical analyst who used to trade stocks and commodities. He wanted to find out the right timing for his trades: when to buy and when to sell. He wanted to find an indicator which could give sufficiently reliable buy and sell signals for a stock or commodity. And for this, he wanted to detect the oversold and overbought levels of a stock.

So, you see, timing the market was the chief purpose behind Wilder's invention of the RSI.

To give more weightage to recent price moves, Wilder uses an exponential moving average for calculating the RSI. This is why the RSI is more smooth and consistent than other indicators, and tends to be less jumpy.

While using the RSI, never forget that its primary function is to tell us when we should buy a stock, and when we should sell it! This is the chief purpose for which it was invented.

Wilder firmly believed that the RSI has the potential to identify, ahead of time, whether a stock is growing stronger or weaker.

The RSI Is a Leading Indicator

Wilder said this about the RSI: "It measure(d) the current strength and weakness of a particular market often in advance of the move."

The RSI is the strength meter of a stock/index, and it is considered a leading indicator.

There are two types of indicators in the stock market: lagging indicators and leading indicators.

Lagging indicators follow the price (like moving averages).

Leading indicators lead prices; that is, the price follows them (like the RSI).

In simple language, it means that the price will usually follow a leading indicator like the RSI, so the movements of the RSI can predict what the price is planning to do.

Of course, like with any other rule, there are exceptions here, too, but the general consensus is that the price usually follows the RSI.

Don't get confused by the full name of the RSI (Relative Strength Index). Always remember that the RSI is not an absolute strength indicator.

In fact, the RSI shows the strength of a stock or index relative to the historical strength of the same stock.

It does not compare any stock's strength with the strength of any other stock, or with the whole stock market. For that purpose, there is another tool called 'Relative Strength', which compares a stock's strength to another stock or index. It is easy to get confused by the similar names, but try to remember that 'Relative Strength' compares two different stocks/indices, while the 'Relative Strength Index' (RSI) compares the strengths of the same stock/index at different time periods.

Now we will move on to the real secrets of the RSI.

The secret of a great dish is in the recipe; likewise, the secret of the RSI is in its unique calculation method.

The calculation method is the soul of the RSI, so we are going to spend some time on it. We will tamper with prices to observe how the RSI moves and see why it reacts the way it does.

In the next chapter, you will know why we find RSI divergences, why it is considered overbought above 70, and why it is considered oversold below 30.

So let us move on to the next chapter, which takes us

to the basics: the calculation method of the RSI, because the real secret of the RSI is in its calculation method.

CHAPTER 3

The Real Secret of the RSI Is in Its Calculation Method

"The trend is your friend UNLESS it is about to end."

— **Thomas DeMark**

The RSI is a momentum oscillator that measures the velocity and magnitude of directional price movements. Momentum means the RATE of the rise or fall in price.

The Closing Price Decides the RSI Level

The RSI is calculated on the basis of the closing price of a bar or candle. If it is a 1-minute chart, the RSI would be calculated at the end of 1 minute; if it is a 1-day chart, the RSI would be calculated with the price at the end of the market close for that day.

On day trading platforms, you can also see RSI levels during live markets, but they are only tentative and are subject to change at the end of the day. So if you are trading on the basis of daily charts, don't act on intraday levels of the RSI, because the RSI is always calculated on the closing price of a stock or index.

It does not bother about the day highs or lows or the opening (if you are interested in those, you can always look at candlestick charts). The close is the most important price; it is believed that closing price is the final verdict of traders on that day.

The Dilemma of the Closing Price

The RSI is calculated using the closing price of a stock. This poses a unique problem for those traders who trade on the basis of the RSI.

Suppose such a trader gets a signal from the RSI during market hours. But he can't act on it until the market closes, because only then will the RSI give a valid and confirmed signal on the daily chart.

Our trader is frustrated. During market hours, he can see, on Investing.com or some other website, when the RSI has crossed a particular important level. But he is not sure whether the RSI will sustain the movement till the market close. And if he doesn't buy today, the market may gap up tomorrow at opening.

What should he do, in such a case? His worry about a gap up is valid; at important junctures, stocks or index use the gap up method to clear a resistance or to give a message about a trend shift.

In such a case, our trader should keep on watching the live RSI levels on Investing.com (daily values), and he should buy the stock in the last 5 minutes to ensure that the RSI level doesn't change significantly.

Don't hurry to buy on the basis of an intraday RSI signal on a daily chart, as you don't know whether the RSI would be able to maintain that level till the end.

Remember, the RSI only recognises the closing price.

Let's Calculate the RSI

The RSI gives a ratio of gains and losses for a period of 14 days.

If there are more gains, the RSI will be higher (with every gain, the down average comes down, though it may happen that the up average also comes down, if the gains for the day are below the up average).

If there are more losses, the RSI will be lower.

The amount of gains or losses is also important. For example, if a stock closes 10% higher, its RSI would increase more than that stock, which closes only 1% higher.

And one more thing: the RSI is calculated exponentially, so today's gain or loss carries more weight in calculations.

If you want to understand the inside secrets of the RSI, let us check how it is calculated (the calculation sheet is straight from Wilder's book; I have used prices with round figures to make it simple):

Scenario 1: The RSI in an Uptrend									
1	2	3	4	5	6	7	8	9	10
Day	Close	Up	Down	Up Avg.	Down Avg.	5/6'	1+(7)'	100/8'	100-9'
1	80								
2	100	20	0						
3	120	20	0						
4	140	20	0						
5	160	20	0						
6	180	20	0						
7	200	20	0						
8	220	20	0						
9	240	20	0						
10	260	20	0						
11	240	0	20						
12	260	20	0						
13	280	20	0						
14	300	20	0						
15	320	20	0	18.57	1.43	13	14	7.14	92.86
16	340	20	0	18.67	1.33	14.08	15.08	6.63	93.37
17	360	20	0	18.77	1.23	15.24	16.24	6.16	93.84
18	380	20	0	18.86	1.14	16.49	17.49	5.72	94.28
19	400	20	0	18.94	1.06	17.83	18.83	5.31	94.69
20	420	20	0	19.01	0.99	19.28	20.28	4.93	95.07

In Scenario 1, this stock had only one down day. All the others were up days. So the trend is definitely UP.

Look at the increase in RSI levels. It is getting slower and slower as it moves further up.

It will look like a 'flattening of the curve' on the RSI panel. You see, on a price scale of 0–100, the progress of the RSI will be sharper in its zoneless area, rather than in the zones.

This flattening of the curve is mostly seen in the overbought/oversold zones of the RSI. In the case of an uptrend, this flattening happens because prices are increasing, but they are not increasing sharply or more than the up average of the RSI. This RSI flattening indicates that momentum is not increasing, or that the RATE of positive price change has decreased.

A flattening of the curve doesn't necessarily mean that the price will reverse immediately; it more often means that the RSI is going to reverse. It has to, because momentum is falling.

See, the RATE of positive price change should be going up consistently. If it stalls, it will result in a flattening of the RSI curve.

In this scenario, you can observe that from Day 16 to Day 20, the consistent gains of Rs. 20 increased the RSI levels to 0.51, 0.48, 0.44, 0.4, and 0.38 respectively. The momentum of the RSI is definitely slowing down. And this is because the RATE of positive price change is not consistently increasing.

Besides, the RSI always slows down above 70 or below 30 for trending prices. If the price is mildly increasing, the RSI may hardly move above 80. What is the reason?

The reason is that if the price increases only mildly, its up average will come down.

The higher the RSI goes, the higher the gains it needs to push up further. It is a momentum oscillator, so the momentum has to keep increasing to make it increase. If the momentum slows down (indicated by the up average), the RSI would also slow down.

The RSI Has an Anti-Trend Bias at Extreme Zones

The RSI typically reacts very wildly to anti-trend prices around overbought or oversold zones.

But if you are a beginner, you should know what a trend is first. Trends can be broadly divided into two major types: primary and secondary (we are not counting minor trends, which come under secondary trends; Elliott Waves are nothing but trends within trends at regular intervals).

A primary trend is defined with the help of a trendline or a moving average. General consensus is that if the price of a stock or index is above its 200 DMA (200-day moving average), the primary trend is bullish or up. If the price of a stock or index is below its 200 DMA, its primary trend is bearish or down. See the picture below:

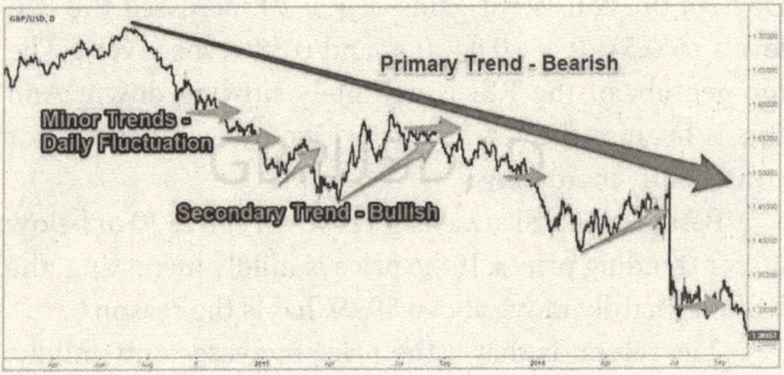

It is very important to know how the RSI reacts to price changes in the direction of the primary trend, and how it reacts to price changes against the direction of the primary trend (for the sake of simplicity, we will call it an anti-trend).

To check this, we will just make a slight change to Scenario 1 and see the reaction of the RSI to an anti-trend price movement.

The table given is the same as that which was given above. We have only changed the price of Day 20 and put a loss of Rs. 20 instead of a gain of Rs. 20.

Let us see what sort of reaction the RSI would give in this scenario (Scenario 2). Please compare the Day 20 RSI movement in Scenario 2 with that of Scenario 1.

Scenario 2: Anti-Trend Bias									
1	2	3	4	5	6	7	8	9	10
Day	Close	Up	Down	Up Avg.	Down Avg.	5/6'	1+(7)'	100/8'	100-9'
1	80								
2	100	20	0						
3	120	20	0						
4	140	20	0						
5	160	20	0						
6	180	20	0						
7	200	20	0						
8	220	20	0						
9	240	20	0						
10	260	20	0						
11	240	0	20						
12	260	20	0						
13	280	20	0						
14	300	20	0						
15	320	20	0	18.57	1.43	13.00	14.00	7.14	92.86
16	340	20	0	18.67	1.33	14.08	15.08	6.63	93.37
17	360	20	0	18.77	1.23	15.24	16.24	6.16	93.84
18	380	20	0	18.86	1.14	16.49	17.49	5.72	94.28
19	400	20	0	18.94	1.06	17.83	18.83	5.31	94.69
20	380	0	20	17.59	2.41	7.28	8.28	12.07	87.93

Here, the price has moved against the primary trend, which is UP. The overall trend is bullish, but this day close is bearish. See for yourself: on a gain of Rs. 20, the RSI barely moved on Day 19—by just 0.4—to 94.68. But on Day 20, it crashed 7 full points to 87.92, though the price difference was the same (the only difference was that it was anti-trend instead of pro-trend).

Why so?

There is a logic behind it.

Pay attention to column 6, 'Down Average', where, on Day 20, the down average became more than double and jumped to 2.41.

So whenever you look at a chart, always remember that the RSI gives slow movements on trending prices and fast movements on anti-trend prices, especially in overbought and oversold territories. And the reason behind it is the interplay of the up average and down average.

If a stock is rising continuously, a small fall will move the RSI disproportionately by higher points.

Likewise, if a stock is falling continuously, a small rise will move RSI disproportionately by higher points.

This is the real cause of price/RSI divergences, which we will explore later on.

Want to experiment further?

The Size of the Gain/Loss Is Important

Now suppose we increase the Day 20 loss from 20 to 80. What will happen in this scenario (Scenario 3)? We have just changed the Day 20 figures, so you can skip looking at the rest of the table.

Scenario 3: The Size of the Gain/Loss Is Important									
1	2	3	4	5	6	7	8	9	10
Day	Close	Up	Down	Up Avg.	Down Avg.	5/6'	1+(7)'	100/8'	100-9'
1	80								
2	100	20	0						
3	120	20	0						
4	140	20	0						
5	160	20	0						
6	180	20	0						
7	200	20	0						
8	220	20	0						
9	240	20	0						
10	260	20	0						
11	240	0	20						
12	260	20	0						
13	280	20	0						
14	300	20	0						
15	320	20	0	18.57	1.43	13.00	14.00	7.14	92.86
16	340	20	0	18.67	1.33	14.08	15.08	6.63	93.37
17	360	20	0	18.77	1.23	15.24	16.24	6.16	93.84
18	380	20	0	18.86	1.14	16.49	17.49	5.72	94.28
19	400	20	0	18.94	1.06	17.83	18.83	5.31	94.69
20	320	0	80	17.59	6.70	2.62	3.62	27.59	72.41

See the jump in the down average (it jumps a whopping six times) and the corresponding big change in the RSI levels. The RSI falls no less than 22 points; can you believe it? It happened because the anti-trend momentum sharply became stronger. And the RSI is a momentum oscillator.

So remember, the quantum, or the size of the fall, is

important. And it is also important to check whether the price is moving in the direction of the trend or against it.

And don't forget to check the Day 15 and Day 20 figures. The price on both these days is the same—320—but see the difference in the RSI levels!

> **An Interesting Fact**
>
> Can a stock touch an RSI level of 100? Yes—if it is continuously on an upper circuit since its listing, as its down average would be 0. For example, Ruchi Soya has had an RSI level of 100 since February 2020 because after its relisting, there has not been a single down day, so its down average is 0.
>
> The price of Ruchi Soya was around 35 in February 2020, but due to continuous upper circuits, it zoomed to 480 levels as of May 6, 2020, and the upper circuit button is still on.

The Secret of Divergence Is in Calculation

Unless you happen to have the tastes of Warren Buffett or Charlie Munger, spreadsheets may seem boring to you, so pardon me for this—I would like to show you just one more spreadsheet, which will show you how a divergence happens between the RSI and the price.

In simple language, a divergence means that the price and the RSI are going in opposite directions; either the price is going up and the RSI is declining (around overbought levels), or the price is going down and the RSI is increasing (around oversold levels).

In technical terms, there are more requirements (to reduce confusion, I am giving a bullish trend scenario; you can apply this to bearish trend scenarios).

Technical Requirements for a Bullish Divergence

1. The price makes a new recent low, P1 (not an all-time low, but the lowest valley on the recent chart). The RSI also makes a new low, R1.
2. The price gives at least one green candle in the opposite direction, P2 (that means a bullish candle in a bearish trend).
3. The price makes another new low, P3, below its recent low.
4. The RSI fails to reach or cross the level of its previous low, R1.

Now see for yourself how a price/RSI divergence takes place in the spreadsheet.

Technical Requirements for a Bearish Divergence

1. The price makes a new recent high, P1 (not an all-time high, but the top peak on the recent chart). The RSI also makes a new high, R1.
2. The price gives at least one red candle in the opposite direction, P2 (that means a bearish candle in a bullish trend).

3. The price makes another new high, P3, above its recent high.
4. The RSI fails to reach or cross the level of its previous high, R1.

This is RSI bearish divergence in a nutshell.

Scenario 4: Why Does Price/RSI Divergence Happen?									
1	2	3	4	5	6	7	8	9	10
Day	Close	Up	Down	Up Avg.	Down Avg.	5/6'	1+(7)'	100/8'	100-9'
1	80								
2	100	20	0						
3	120	20	0						
4	140	20	0						
5	160	20	0						
6	180	20	0						
7	200	20	0						
8	220	20	0						
9	240	20	0						
10	260	20	0						
11	240	0	20						
12	260	20	0						
13	280	20	0						
14	300	20	0						
15	320	20	0	18.57	1.43	13.00	14.00	7.14	92.86
16	340	20	0	18.67	1.33	14.08	15.08	6.63	93.37
17	320	0	20	17.34	2.66	6.52	7.52	13.30	86.70
18	350	30	0	18.24	2.47	7.39	8.39	11.93	88.07
19	320	0	30	16.94	4.44	3.82	4.82	20.75	79.25
20	360	40	0	18.59	4.12	4.51	5.51	18.14	81.86

In the above spreadsheet (Scenario 4), you can see at a glance that the stock is in a clear uptrend and the price is rising most days. No wonder its RSI is above 90 on the 15th day.

On Day 16, the stock gains Rs. 20 and makes a new high of 340. Notice the RSI level (93.36), as it will be useful when we discuss RSI divergence. As the stock is in an uptrend, there is not much impact on the up average, so the RSI gives only a modest increase of 0.51.

On Day 17, the price declines by Rs. 20 (the same price difference as on Day 16), but as this movement is against the prevailing trend, it makes a significant impact on the down average. That's why the RSI declines by a full 7 points. Look at column 6, 'Down Average'. On Day 16, it was merely 1.32, but it doubled on Day 17. No wonder the RSI gave such a drastic reaction!

On Day 18, the price increases by Rs. 30 and the stock makes a new high of 350. Check the RSI level (88.07); it is less than Day 16's RSI level. The price has made a new high, but the RSI didn't make a new high, and gave a lesser reading. This is divergence number 1. By the way, price/RSI divergences occur due to disproportionate anti-trend reactions of the RSI.

On Day 19, the price declines by Rs. 30—and look! Column 6, 'Down Average', increases substantially, and hence the RSI gives a sharp reaction by declining by a whopping 9 points.

On Day 20, the price increases by 40 and the stock makes a new high of 360. However, check the RSI level here in the last column (it is 81.85). Here, the stock has made a new high, but the RSI didn't make a new high, so here we have divergence number 2.

As they say, a picture is worth more than a thousand words, so here I'm giving two charts related to Scenario 4: RSI Divergence. They will tell you the whole story at a single glance.

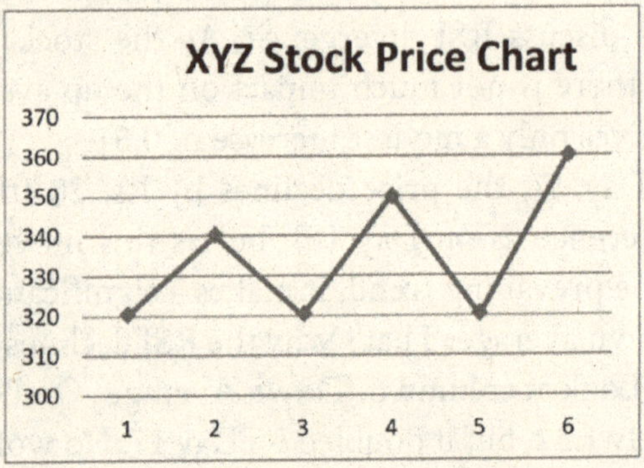

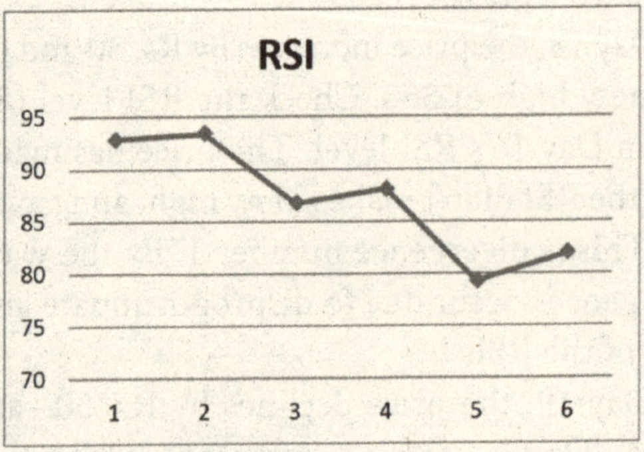

Now observe the three new highs in the table below to understand the concept of divergence more clearly (and remember that a bearish candle exists between these new highs according to technical requirements).

Divergence	Day	The price makes a new high	The RSI doesn't make a new high
NIL, as there are no previous RSI readings to compare	Day 16	340	93.37
1	Day 18	350	88.07
2	Day 20	360	81.85

Do you understand what is happening in this price/RSI divergence scenario?

The price is making higher highs, while the RSI is going down.

A price/RSI divergence means the primary trend is becoming weaker, and the secondary trend is becoming stronger.

It means that momentum is slowing down.

It means that bulls are losing their power and bears are getting stronger.

This is why it is said that divergences predict trend reversals well in advance.

Remember, a divergence does not guarantee trend reversal; it merely indicates the possibility of trend reversal—or, as Cardwell and his followers point out, the possibility of retracement. Whether it is a reversal or a retracement, it just means that the direction of the price may change soon.

Important Tip

The RSI is a mathematically biased indicator, and its bias is anti-trend when it is near overbought and oversold levels. It is most unbiased when it oscillates between the index values of 40 and 60.

The levels of RSI divergences are as follows:

RSI Bearish Divergence	Levels 60–80
RSI Bullish Divergence	Levels 20–40

Important Tip

If you want to compare the movements of the price and the RSI more accurately, look not at the candlestick chart, but at the LINE chart of the stock.

In a line chart, it is easier to compare the slopes and angles of both lines.

When you compare one line (price) with another line (RSI), it is like comparing oranges with oranges.

When you compare candlesticks with an RSI line, it is like comparing cucumbers with oranges.

Note: Candlesticks have their own significance, but for the purpose of RSI comparison, it is somewhat better to also check line charts.

Like this:

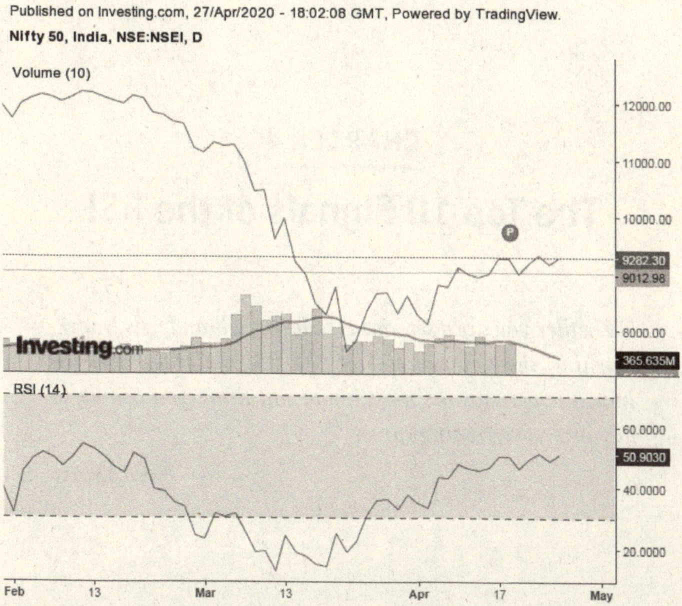

If you observe the price line and the RSI line in the above chart, you will notice at a glance that there is bullish divergence at the bottom. The RSI has peaked before the price and given a signal of a trend change.

Now that we understand the typical RSI calculation methodology, which clarifies divergence signals, let us move on to the next chapter, where we will briefly discuss other significant signals given by the RSI.

CHAPTER 4

The Top 10 Signals of the RSI

"Whether you are a seasoned trader, or a brand new trader, learning the key concepts of the RSI, Relative Strength Index, is perhaps the most important thing you can do to advance your trading career."

— **Paul Dean**

In this chapter, we will discuss RSI signals, which can be used for trading purposes. Let us now briefly discuss them with the help of charts.

1. Tops and Bottoms (Top at 70 and Bottom at 30)

According to Wilder, tops and bottoms are indicated when the RSI goes above 70 or below 30. This is called a vanilla trading strategy, which is discussed in Chapter 9.

According to Wilder, "The Index will usually top out or bottom out before the actual market top or bottom, giving an indication that a reversal or at least a significant reaction is imminent."

The RSI gives an indication of overbought and oversold conditions, so the simplest thing in the world would be to buy a stock when its RSI reverses from level 30 and sell it when its RSI reverses from level 70. Simple as clockwork!

Yet it is not that simple. The RSI doesn't dutifully travel straight to the opposite line, but, at times, it reverses in between to touch the same line again.

As you can see in the chart given below, the price is in a downtrend. Pay attention to the RSI on the bottom panel. It regularly shuttles from the oversold zone (30) to the overbought zone (70), though, at times, it reverses its course in between. Here, the dotted line on the top of the RSI panel indicates a level of 70, and the dotted line on the bottom of the panel indicates a level of 30.

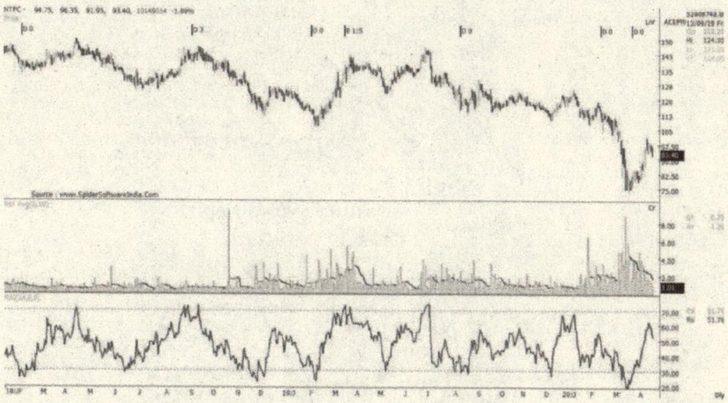

2. Failure Swings

When the RSI does not exceed its previous high at overbought or oversold levels, it is called a failure swing.

Here, the RSI makes a pattern like a slanted M (overbought level) or slanted W (oversold level). In technical terms, it makes a sort of double top or double bottom.

Failure swings are very similar to divergences.

Wilder has pointed out that whenever the RSI gives a failure swing at the top and falls down below its preceding valley, the stock can be sold—or short-sold, rather.

Likewise, whenever the RSI gives a failure swing at the bottom and rises above its preceding peak, the stock can be bought.

Wilder has laid down rules about trading failure swings in his book, as can be seen in the picture given below.

(3) **Failure Swings:** Failure swings above 70 or below 30 are very strong indications of a market reversal. (See Fig. 6.3 and Fig. 6.4.)

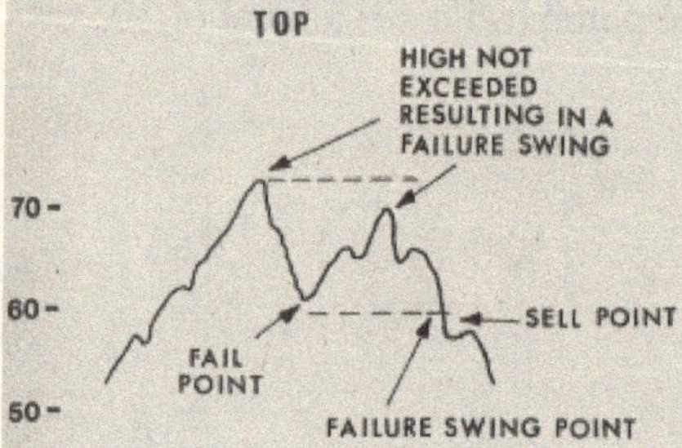

Fig. 6.3

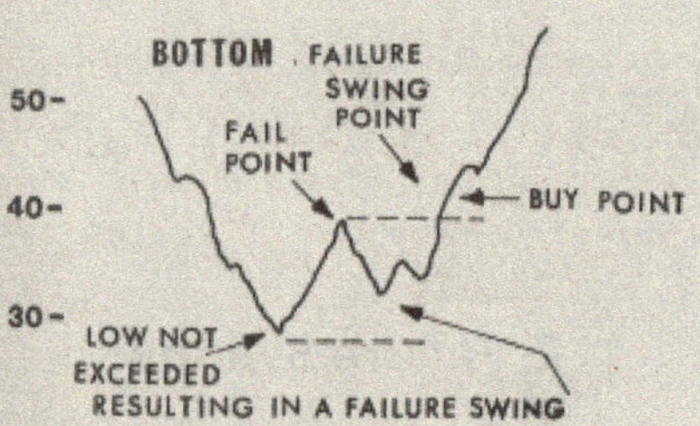

Fig. 6.4

The failure swing signal is confirmed when the RSI drops below the valley in an M-formation, or rises above its preceding peak in a W-formation.

A failure swing is considered more significant when it takes place within oversold or overbought zones.

Note: However, common sense tells us that failure swings often happen outside oversold/overbought zones. Usually, the first peak/valley is inside an oversold/overbought zone, and the second peak or valley is made outside the zone. (As I have already said, this is similar to a divergence, and a failure swing is the way to trade an RSI divergence. There have been several experts, including Cardwell and Hayden and several others, who claim that RSI divergences can't be traded. They failed to see that divergences can be traded, and that a failure swing is the way to trade them.)

Failure swings are, rather, a part of a divergence, and Wilder is using a failure swing to confirm the divergence. Divergences can fail if the RSI retreats from the zone, but turns back soon to enter the zone and exceeds the previous high/low. Wilder is, in fact, saying that if a failure swing is confirmed in the above manner, the risk of the RSI turning back is less, and it should be expected to touch its opposite zone.

As John Hayden points out, "A failure swing occurs when there is either a bearish or bullish divergence... The failure swing is believed to 'confirm' that a market reversal is valid."

3. Support and Resistance

Support and resistance areas often show up on the RSI before they appear on the price panel. By drawing trendlines and channels on the RSI line, we can recognise support and resistance areas on price charts.

- For drawing a resistance trendline, draw a line connecting recent highs of the RSI.
- For drawing a support trendline, draw a line connecting recent lows of the RSI.

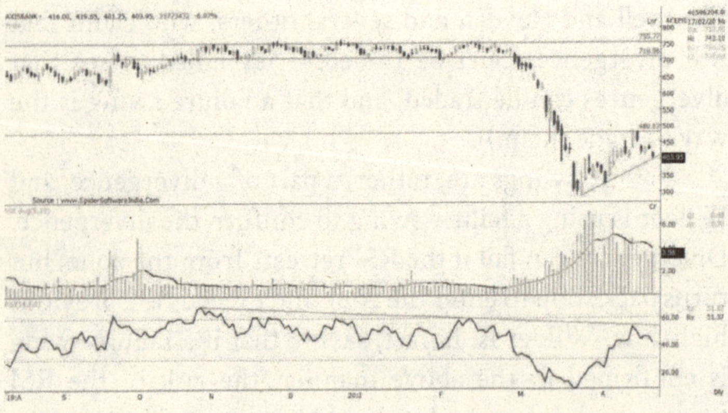

In the above chart, the RSI resistance line has clearly marked the level where the price will stop increasing and reverse.

Note: It is very strange that an indicator's trendline can plot support and resistance areas. You see, most traders don't draw trendlines on the RSI panel. Besides, trendlines are highly subjective and not at all objective like horizontal price levels. So it is quite amazing why and how a support or resistance line on the RSI can predict the future price movements of a stock. Quite incredible!

4. Centreline Crossover

If the RSI line crosses the centreline from below to the upside, it means that the average gains are exceeding the average losses now. It signals a bullish momentum shift, and this is why it is considered to be a good buy signal.

On the other hand, if the RSI line crosses the centreline from above to the downside, it means that the average losses are exceeding the average gains. It signals a bearish momentum shift, and this is why it is considered to be a good sell signal.

An RSI line of 50 is considered to be a support and resistance in itself.

When the RSI rallies above 50, it is considered a bullish confirmation; when it falls below 50, it is seen as a bearish confirmation.

50 is considered to be the middle territory of the RSI, as it falls in the exact middle of the 0–100 and 30–70 ranges. However, in the case of Cardwell's range shifts, the 50 level ceases to be the exact middle, as you will see in the next point.

In a bull market, the centreline (50) provides multiple low-risk buying opportunities, as the RSI spends most of the time in the 50–70 range.

In a bear market, the centreline (50) provides multiple shorting opportunities, as the RSI spends most of the time in the 50–30 range.

5. Range Shift (Trend Change Signal)

Wilder's normal range for the RSI was 30–70; when the RSI was below 30, it was considered oversold; when the RSI was above 70, it was considered overbought.

However, Andrew Cardwell modified this original theory by proclaiming that the 30–70 range was not universal.

Cardwell noticed that in uptrends, the RSI usually maintains levels of 40–80, while it maintains levels of 20–60 in downtrends. Cardwell observed that when securities change from an uptrend to a downtrend and vice versa, the RSI will undergo a 'range shift'.

- **Normal range:** 30–70
- **Bull range:** 40–80
- **Bear range:** 20–60

This idea is psychologically tenable. A range shift takes place due to fear and greed.

In a bull market, when a stock corrects, the left-out investors turn greedy and rush in early to buy the stock and move it up, so the RSI doesn't fall to its normal range of 30.

And in a bull market, when a stock reaches the overbought levels of 70, nobody is in a hurry to book profits, as the stock is rising every day. When there is no serious selling, the RSI goes on to touch level 80, as its up average is consistently going up and its down average is consistently going down (remember our calculation sheets).

As Andrew Cardwell puts it, "So the RSI to me is an ideal indicator because it's incorporating not only price and momentum but it can also be used as a sentiment tool to see when most people are bullish, they get excited, it's going to go through the 70 level. When it corrects, it's not going to correct all the way down to 30. It will come near 40 and those who missed the train first out of the station are more apt to jump on it because by then you've established enough of a trend."

In a bear market, people are more afraid to buy, so they don't purchase the stock at the 30 level; there is no hurry, as the stock is falling every day. You see, here, the down average is increasing every day and the up average is going down, so the RSI goes below 30 easily.

In a bear market, when the RSI rises and reaches near the 60 level, traders are overcome with fear that its price may fall at any time, so they want to book profits in a hurry, otherwise they will miss the boat.

As Constance Brown puts it, "The general rule to follow for a bear market is that RSI will oscillate within a range of 20 to 30 at the low end of the scale up to an upper resistance zone of 55 to 65. This is true regardless of market or time horizon."

As I have said, theoretically, the concept of range shifts is all right.

However, range shifts don't work much in the Indian market—at least not in the daily charts of Nifty or its 50 companies. We observe that in almost all daily charts, the RSI regularly touches 30 in bull markets, too. And it does not touch 80 so often in daily charts.

Maybe Cardwell and Constance Brown were talking

about another timeframe (weekly or monthly charts instead of daily charts), or maybe they were talking about another market (forex or commodities instead of stocks).

Remember, monthly charts are slow. In April 2020, Nifty's monthly RSI was 31.92 (after the 30% quick crash), and it was the lowest reading after 1996. Even during the 2008 bear market, the lowest reading of Nifty's monthly RSI was 35.47, so Cardwell's range shift doesn't apply there, either.

Cardwell's research might have shown range shifts working in certain markets, but it seems that the Indian stock market still follows Wilder and his 30–70 rule in daily timeframes.

Cardwell's concept of range shifts may be true of lesser timeframes or minute charts (I myself have once done a trade on this basis in 1-minute charts).

In the daily charts of Nifty stocks, the evidence of range shifts was lacking; they kept on shuttling between 70 and 30 almost regularly, whether they were in an uptrend or a downtrend.

Perhaps the logic behind the range shift is that a stock turns bearish due to bearish divergence of the RSI, which should necessarily take place below the previous top, and therefore 60 is the ideal place for the RSI to turn back.

Important Finding: In my research on daily charts of Nifty stocks, I observed that during downtrends, stocks dip deeper below 30; during uptrends, stocks tend to cross far above 70. It is not necessary to touch the 20 or 80 levels, but they tend to go deeper than usual in the overbought/oversold zones.

If a stock is in a downtrend, it is obviously weak. The reason is that there is more selling going on rather than buying. So its momentum is weak, and when momentum is weak, we can't expect the RSI to touch the 70 level on the upside, and we should expect the RSI to breach the 30 line rather more frequently.

Let us see a weekly chart of Coal India, where the range shift applies to a large extent. At the left hand, on the RSI panel, you can observe that it was above 70 (actually, it was on 78), then, during the downturn, it fell down below the 20 level. Then it turned up and reached the 60 level, but couldn't touch the 70 line. It tried to touch 70 again and again, but couldn't succeed. To be fair, it didn't fall to the 20 level, either. So let us disallow this range shift rule in the Indian context.

Now look at the chart of Coal India (remember, this is a weekly chart).

- The top dotted line on the RSI panel represents the 70 level.
- The second top dotted line represents the 60 level.
- And the dotted line at the bottom represents the 30 level.

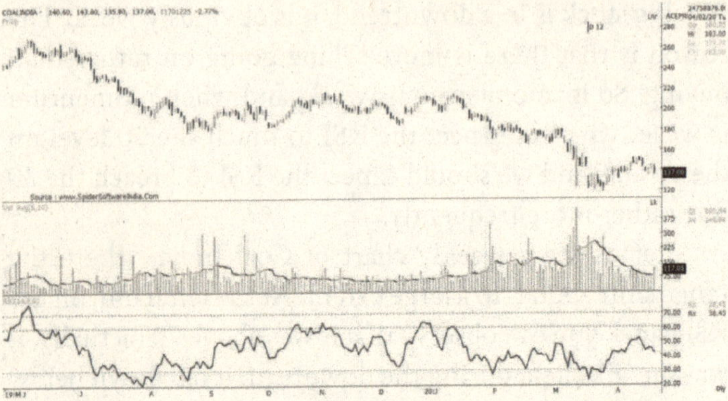

In the above chart, you can see that the RSI was above 70 initially. Then it went below 30 and subsequently recovered, but for the rest of the period, it could not reach above the 60 level, indicating that Coal India had turned bearish and shifted its normal trading range.

- If the RSI cannot push above the 60 level, then there is weakness in the market. If the RSI cannot go down below the 40 level, then there is strength in the market.
- If the RSI retraces from 70 and remains above 50, it shows a bullish trend. In fact, it indicates that it is making room for further bullish movement of the price.
- Likewise, if the RSI rises from 30 and remains below 50, it shows a bearish trend.

The range shift of the RSI warns of potential trend changes. It predicts that the trend is going to change, as momentum has shifted.

The range shift gives us another significant clue. It tells us that when the RSI crosses the 60 level on the upside, it starts a bullish rally, and we should not expect this rally to end when the RSI reaches level 70.

As per Paul Dean, any time the price is trending down, the trader should be watching for upward range shifts, and when the price is trending up, the trader should look for downward range shifts. The shorter the trading timeframe, the more often this will happen.

Perhaps the key to the mystery of range shifts lies in Paul Dean's statement above. This rule of range shift may—just may—be applied to minute charts. But day traders needn't bother; this rule is not for you. This range shift rule is for short-term charts—or rather, minute charts.

As I have already said in the beginning, a serious study about the RSI in an Indian context has never been done, so we don't exactly know which theories work here and which don't. Now we have seen that the theory of range shifts doesn't work in an Indian context—at least in daily charts.

6. Channels and Trendlines

You can draw trendlines and channels on the RSI panel, too, just as you do on the price panel.

The RSI trendlines can also be drawn to work as resistance and support lines. This way, you would have a good idea of stock support and resistance levels. It may also help in profit booking.

The RSI gives trendline and channel breakouts, too (I have discussed it at length in my previous Kindle book,

How To See a Breakout Before It Really Happens: Breakout Signals in Descending Channels).

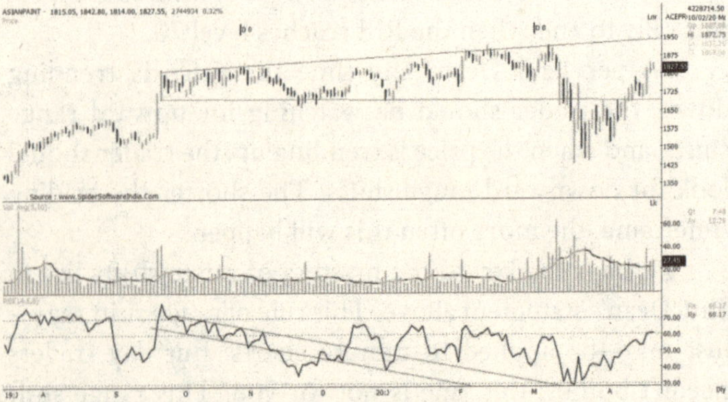

The general rule of channels is that if a stock is running in a channel, you should draw an identical channel on the RSI, so that you can compare the two channels and observe any deviations.

However, RSI experts advise that we should make RSI channels in the opposite direction of the price trend (as you can see above). During downtrends, draw ascending channels; during uptrends, draw descending channels. The RSI has limited moving space, from 0–100, so it will have to move out of its channel, and this channel shift can give you a signal about the bearishness or bullishness of the stock. Walter J. Baeyens, in particular, advises using RSI channels to give buy and sell signals.

7. Chart Patterns (Triangles, Head and Shoulders, Inverted H&S, etc.)

On the RSI panel, you can see several candlestick patterns like head and shoulders, pennants, and triangles, and you can trade them just like you do them on price charts. As Wilder puts it, "The Index will display graphic chart formations which may not be obvious on a corresponding bar chart. For instance, head and shoulders, tops or bottoms, pennants or triangles often show up on the index to indicate breakouts and buy and sell points." It means that the RSI can predict breakouts well in advance.

Some of these patterns are what Wilder calls chart formations:

- Say the RSI makes higher highs, higher lows. This indicates that the momentum is rising and that buy strength is more than sell strength. However, at some point, it may stop doing this and will give either a divergence or a reversal signal.
- Say the RSI makes lower highs, lower lows. This indicates that the momentum is slowing down and that selling pressure is more than the buying pressure. However, at some point, it may also signal either a divergence or a reversal.
- Say the RSI makes a head and shoulders pattern (bearish) or an inverted head and shoulders pattern (bullish). The concept and trading rules are the same as on price charts; however, these pattern can be observed more frequently on the RSI panel than on the price panel, because H&S

is valid only on peaks and inverted H&S is valid only in valleys. The price doesn't make peaks and valleys as often as the RSI does. So watch out for a head and shoulders pattern (around level 70), or its opposite, the inverted head and shoulders pattern (around level 30), on the RSI panel.

If you don't have an idea of what a head and shoulders pattern looks like, see the picture given below.

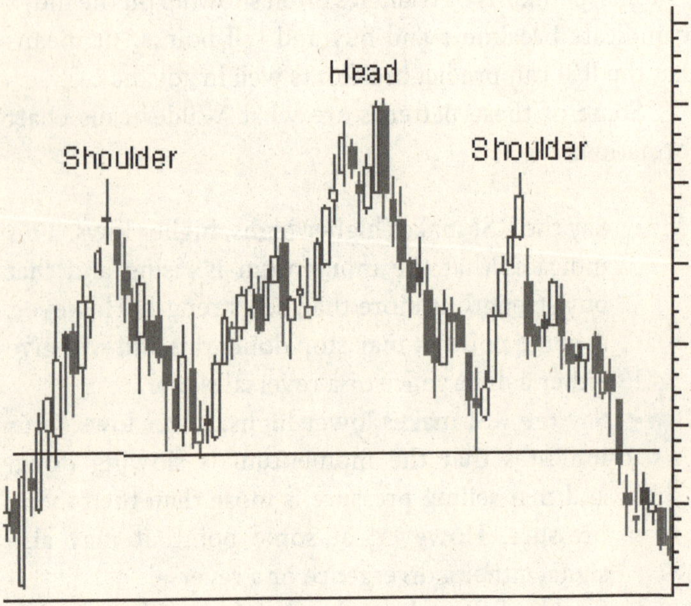

An inverted head and shoulders pattern is just the opposite of a head and shoulders pattern, as you can see in the picture below.

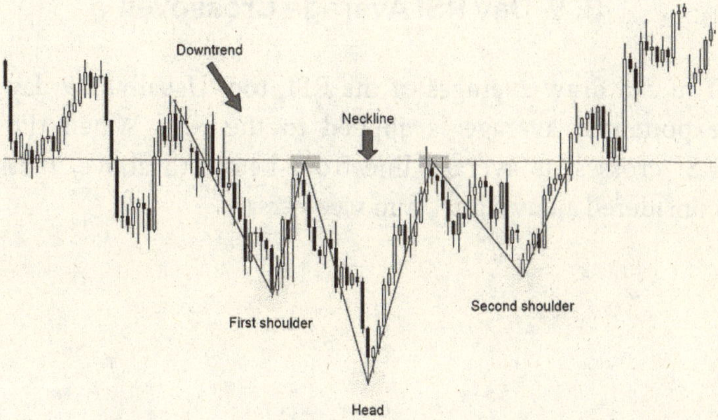

- The RSI makes a double top or double bottom. The RSI can make double tops at level 70 or double bottoms at level 30 to indicate trend reversals even before they happen. And the beauty of it is that while making such patterns, the RSI also gives a divergence. At a double top, it gives a bearish divergence, which indicates that the bullish trend is over, or at least on hold for some time. At a double bottom, it gives a bullish divergence, which indicates that the bearish trend is over, or at least that it is time for some retracement.
- The RSI makes triangles. RSI triangles are often centered around the 50 level, indicating indecision about the future direction. At some point, the RSI breaks out of the triangle one way or the other, and there is a swift move in both the RSI and the price in the near future. And this is as it should be. When momentum shifts, price has to shift as well, as momentum is the power or fuel behind significant price moves.

8. 9-Day RSI Average Crossover

You can draw averages of the RSI, too. Usually, a 9-day exponential average is applied to the RSI. When the RSI crosses its average line from below to above, it is considered a buy signal, and vice versa.

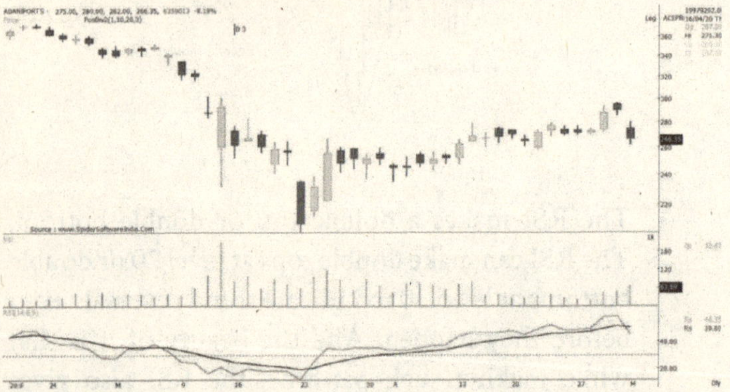

This average line is just an additional helping tool, as it compares the current RSI level with its previous exponential 9-day average. However, this crossover should not be the basis of trading, as the RSI can change tracks after giving a little breakout or breakdown. So it should be confirmed with other bullish or bearish signals or patterns.

Cardwell suggests using a 9-period SMA (simple moving average) and 45-period WMA (weighted moving average) of the RSI to find out the short-term and intermediate trend. If the 9-period SMA is above the 45-period WMA, it is bullish.

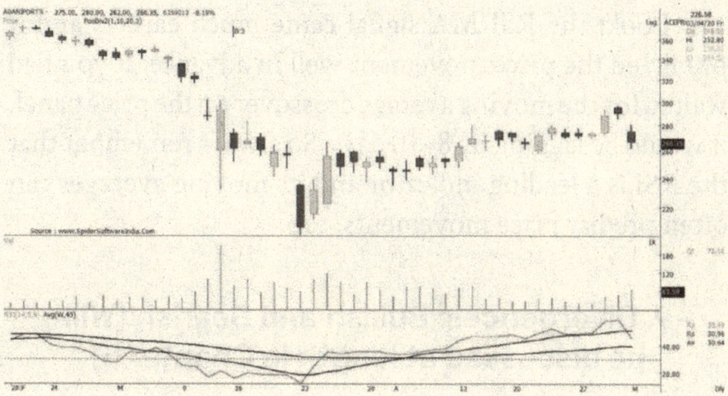

You can experiment here and enhance your learning. If you are drawing a moving average on the price panel, do the same on the RSI panel (the same moving average; for example, if you are drawing a 20 DMA on the price panel, draw a 20 DMA on the RSI panel as well) and check the results. This may tell you something more about the price-RSI relation.

I am giving an example of an Adani Port chart, which we have been using in this section:

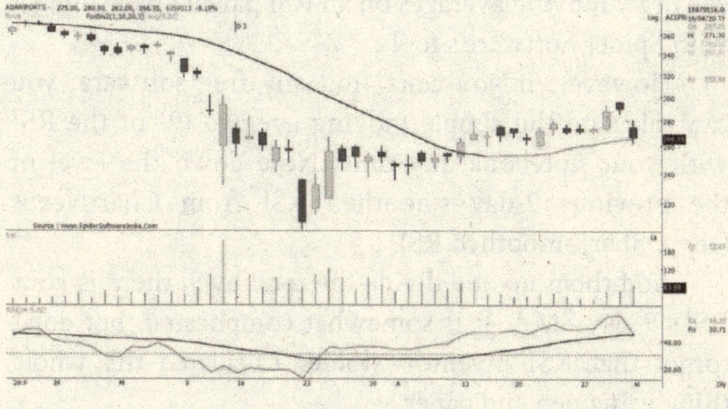

Look: the RSI MA signal came much earlier, and it predicted the price movement well in advance. If you had waited for the moving average crossover on the price panel, it would be lagging by 8–10 days. So always remember that the RSI is a leading indicator and its moving averages can often predict price movements, too.

9. Divergences: Bullish and Bearish (Will be discussed at length in Chapter 5)

10. Reversals: Positive and Negative (Will be discussed at length in Chapter 6)

So, in this chapter, we have learnt about the top 10 signals of the RSI—or rather the top 8 signals of the RSI, as we have yet to go through divergences and reversals, which are considered to be the most powerful signals of the RSI.

After reading the next two chapters, you will complete your RSI signal study and you can try them with your system. I don't know of any free software on which you can draw moving averages on an RSI panel; I have done it with Spider Software's tools.

However, if you can't find any free software, you can calculate the simple moving average (9) of the RSI with your notebook any time. Note down the level of the previous 9-day smoothed RSI from ChartNexus (remember, smoothed RSI) .

Add them up and divide the total by 9; there is your RSI's 9-day SMA. It is somewhat complicated, but don't forget that RSI inventor Wilder calculated the whole thing using pen and paper.

CHAPTER 5

Divergences: Bullish and Bearish

"Divergence is the single most indicative characteristic of the Relative Strength Index."

— J. Welles Wilder

As Wilder puts it, "Divergence between price action and the RSI is a very strong indicator of a market turning point. Divergence occurs when the RSI is increasing and the price movement is either flat or decreasing. Conversely, divergence occurs when the RSI is decreasing and price movement is either flat or increasing."

What Is a Divergence?

Divergence means non-confirmation—the price is moving in a way which is not supported by the RSI.

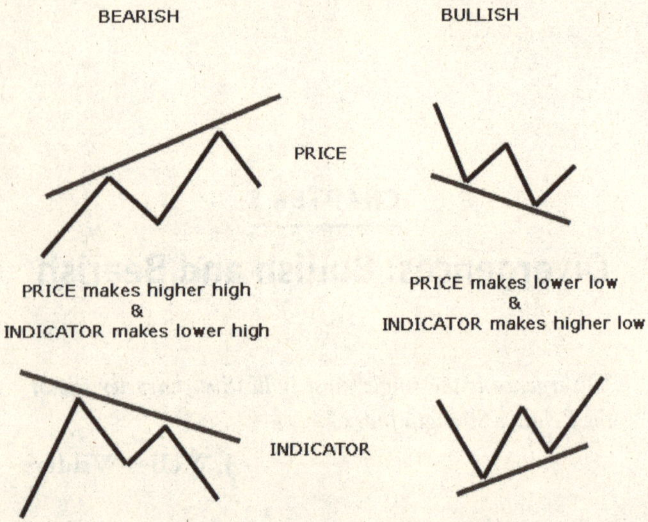

As you can observe in the above picture:

- Bearish divergence occurs when the price makes a higher high and the RSI makes a lower high.
- Bullish divergence occurs when the price makes a lower low and the RSI makes a higher low.

Usually, divergences are to be found at the extreme end of the RSI scale. Bearish divergences are to be found around the 70 level, and bullish divergences are to be found around the 30 level.

There is a positive divergence if the price chart still shows lower bottoms while the opposite occurs in the RSI chart line. This is a sign that the strength and momentum of the falling price movement is decreasing – at least temporarily – and thus increasing the likelihood of an interim price upturn.

Bullish Divergence	Made at the bottom, made in a bearish trend, bullish signal	The price makes new lows, the RSI makes higher lows
Bearish Divergence	Made at the top, made in bullish trend, bearish signal	The price makes new highs, the RSI makes lower lows

To make it easy for you, I will reproduce here the pictures which you have already seen in the chapter on calculation.

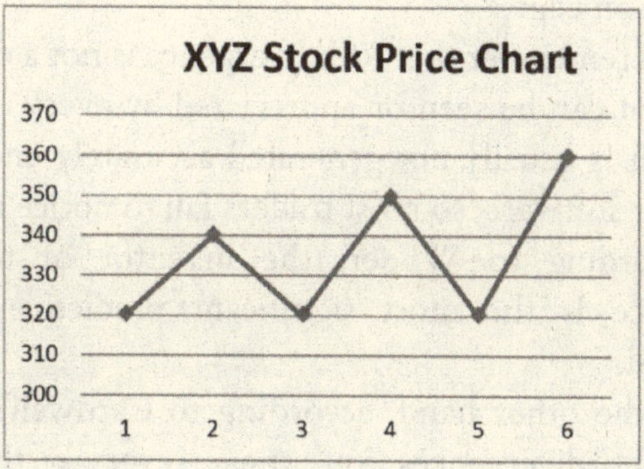

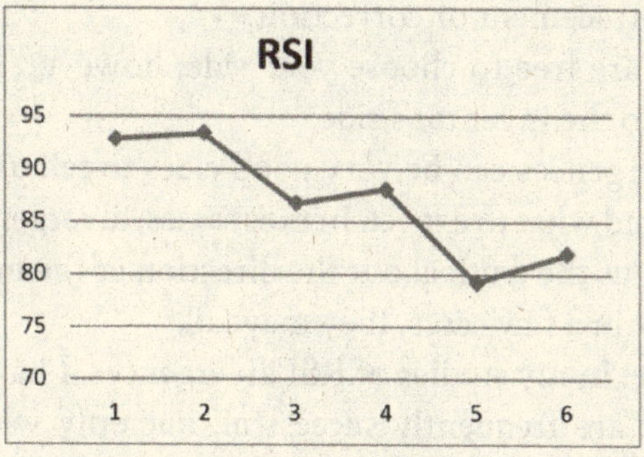

Theory 1: Divergences Are Very Powerful Signals

RSI divergence is a signal that the RSI has reached overbought/oversold levels, and it is also a signal that the momentum is changing and the current trend is weakening.

Divergence is one of the most powerful signals of the RSI. Due to its anti-trend bias, the RSI alerts traders about the possibility of trend reversal, or at least retracement.

As Paul Dean observes, "Divergences act like little spies alerting you to events before they happen so that you will have an edge."

Also remember that RSI divergence is not a common signal that can be seen or appreciated by every technical analyst. It is usually not generated accurately enough by computer software, so most traders fail to notice it.

According to Wilder, the inventor of the RSI, divergence is the most significant predictive feature of the RSI.

On the other hand, according to Cardwell's school of thought, divergences don't mean reversals; they only signify retracement or correction.

You are free to choose your side; however, I will be sticking to the inventor's side.

Divergences can be very good clues to tell us what is coming and what to expect. In most cases, divergences may be telling us the truth about the direction of the market or stock, but in a few cases, they may fail.

Note: In my studies of RSI divergences, I have found that they are frequently successful, but only when they are found at the top or bottom of the price panel. If you observe RSI divergence in the middle of the panel, it may not be a powerful signal. Meaning that for a trend reversal, firstly, it is necessary to have a solid and powerful trend. The stronger the trend, the more powerful an RSI divergence signal would be.

Divergences have meaning only at the top/bottom of the price panel; they don't mean much during the consolidation period, as they are not found on the top or bottom of the price panel at such times, but in between. In my studies, I have found that in such cases, RSI divergence didn't immediately give results.

Theory 2: Divergences Are Minor Signals

Cardwell says, "Both Bullish and Bearish Divergence usually cause a brief price correction and not an actual trend reversal."

According to him, divergence is a minor signal. He demotes the brainchild of his teacher Wilder to promote his own brainchild: reversals. Cardwell says that positive and negative reversals are powerful signals, like dynamite—the true power of the RSI.

Cardwell's school holds the opinion that price/RSI divergence is not an exceptional signal. It occurs frequently, as it is inevitable, and does not warrant any special treatment. It is just one way for the RSI to escape its mathematical constraints (remember our anti-trend discussion from Chapter 3).

John Hayden makes fun of divergences by saying, "Going long when a bullish divergence makes its appearance is a certain way to make small profits and generate large losses."

But not in our studies! Our studies have shown that divergences work. However, it should be kept it in mind that it often takes multiple divergences before the trend reverses.

Walter J. Baeyens also belittles divergences and says, "Divergence occurs frequently and it does not have any special significance."

In my opinion, Walter J. Baeyens misses the point completely. Divergences don't—in fact, they can't—occur every fortnight, as trends don't change so fast. A real trend can go on for several months or even years, for that matter.

Perhaps Baeyens is not talking about extreme divergences here, when the price is at the top or bottom. He seems to be talking about minor divergences, when the RSI reaches the 70 or 30 levels (which happens more frequently).

Cardwell noted that bearish divergence: 1) only occurs in uptrends, and 2) mostly only leads to a brief correction instead of a reversal in the trend. Therefore, bearish divergence is a sign confirming an uptrend.

Similarly, according to Cardwell, bullish divergence is a sign confirming a downtrend. Of course, Cardwell was equating bullish divergence with negative reversal and bearish divergence with positive reversal.

What Cardwell doesn't realise is that price/RSI divergences may be common, but the divergence about which Wilder is talking is very uncommon and is seen infrequently.

Real divergences are few and far between, whereas

reversals are more common. Trends don't change every month in the stock market; however, positive or negative reversals can occur every month.

Cardwell's, or rather Cardwell's school's, problem with RSI divergence is simple: in RSI divergence, you can't determine the entry point, exit point, stop-loss, or target of the price objective. Divergence is not an exact trading tool in itself, which is why Cardwell and other traders don't consider it significant.

As Paul Dean sums it up, "A divergence, although tempting to trade, does not give you any target, so it is impossible to determine your Risk Reward Ratio."

Wait for Multiple Divergences!

I have found in my studies that the RSI can give more than one divergence, and frequently does so. This is why you don't rush in to buy after seeing the first divergence. My observation is that the RSI gives at least two divergence signals, and only then does the trend reverse. However, three RSI divergences in close succession are enough to change the direction of the price.

Important Tip

Don't expect that the market will immediately reverse after an RSI divergence. The trend has to slow down first, then stop, and then reverse. All of this takes time.

Now I am showing you a chart where the price retraced after the first divergence, but the trend didn't reverse, and the stock made another new low, giving a second divergence. This will warn you that you shouldn't rush in to buy as soon as you see a divergence, because multiple divergences may arrive.

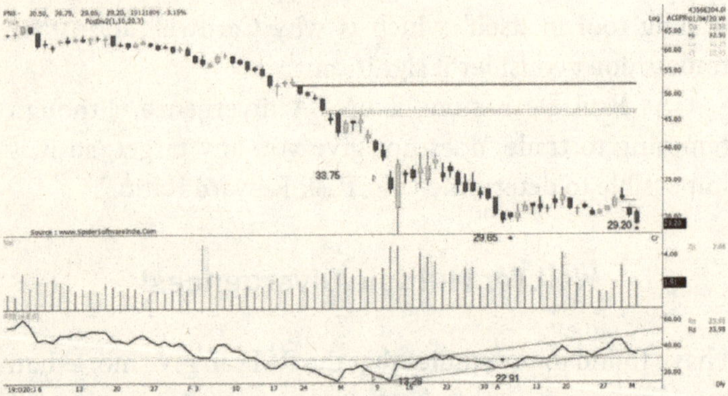

Above, we see the daily chart of PNB, which made a bottom on the price as well as the RSI when the price was at 33.75.

Then the price kept on going lower and made a new low at 29.65. However, the RSI didn't make another low, but was higher than point 1, so there was bullish divergence.

Remember, here, the RSI has made an ascending channel, which it finally breaks when it makes a fresh new low of 29.20 (and there is no need to tell you that the RSI is higher than point 2), so there was bullish divergence number 2 (you can't see the green candle, which came after divergence point 2).

Duration Is Important

This is a reminder that unless you find a divergence in close-by candles, price reversal may need multiple divergences. Far-off divergences are apt to fail, as they tell two different momentum stories. This is why close-by divergence points are considered more powerful.

As John Hayden points out, "The duration of a divergence is important. A two to six day divergence usually indicates that a detour in price is more likely than a longer period. A longer divergence period of weeks and even months, if using daily charts, is usually less indicative that a price detour is coming. The most powerful divergence occurs during a 2 or 3 period divergence."

According to Cardwell, the number of periods between point 1 and point 2 of a divergence are important. The divergences which come within 2–6 periods are more powerful and stronger, whereas divergences found over more than 6 periods are not that significant. This is certainly correct. The nearer the divergence candles, the more powerful the signal, and the swifter the price reaction.

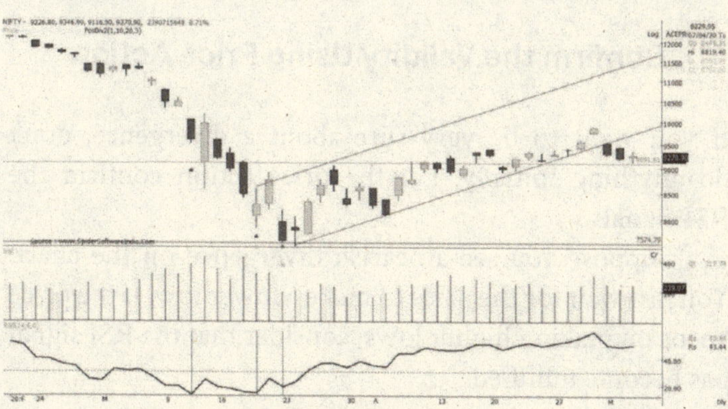

See the above chart of Nifty (Feb-Mar 2020). Here, Nifty is falling down sharply. The price makes a new low (observe the first vertical line from the left on the RSI panel). The RSI also makes a new low. The price falls some more and makes another, but the RSI doesn't make another low and makes a higher low (observe the second vertical line in the middle of the RSI panel). Then, after a green candle, the price makes another lower low. As you can clearly see in the third vertical line from the left, the RSI doesn't make a lower low, but makes a higher low. And soon after, the price reverses. It took two divergences to make it happen.

RSI divergence signals are useful for those who focus primarily on counter-trend strategies. They enable investors to identify changes in trends at a very early stage. However, it remains important to realize that, in many cases, the counter-reaction to the existing trend will be short-lived, and instead of a trend reversal, it may end up as a retracement or correction. That is why they are perhaps better suited to those who like to act a little more aggressively in the very short term.

Confirm the Validity Using Price Action

If you want to be very sure about a divergence, don't do anything initially. Let the price action confirm the RSI signals.

Suppose you see a bearish divergence on the chart. You just wait for the price to make a lower low. If the price keeps on making higher lows, consider that the RSI signal has become nullified.

In my studies, the price often makes a higher high and throws up another RSI divergence. Here, also, try to confirm the signal.

Rule of Thumb

When divergences come, they come in groups of three, or at least two.

When the price makes a lower low, the RSI signal of bearish divergence would be confirmed. This is exactly the concept of a failure swing, which we have already discussed in Chapter 4 (*The Top 10 Signals of the RSI*).

- In the case of a bearish divergence, wait for the price to make a lower low (as it has already made a lower high in the process of giving a divergence).
- In the case of a bullish divergence, wait for the price to make a higher high (as it has made a higher low in the process of giving a divergence).

Remember, whether it is a bearish divergence or bullish divergence, it needs to be confirmed by price action. If the time interval between the diverging candles is smaller, the price would quickly change its course and follow the RSI.

Of course, it may reduce your profit potential to some extent, and you will miss most of the opportunity.

Confirm the Validity Using Candlesticks

This one is for aggressive rather than conservative traders: confirmation by candlestick patterns.

Candlestick patterns, or even a single candle, can also confirm trend reversals.

The following are the most common trend reversal signals found in candlestick charts:

- Morning Star (bullish) and Evening Star (bearish)
- Abandoned Baby
- Doji Star
- Spinning Top
- Hammer
- Bullish Engulfing and Bearish Engulfing

If you find them soon after a divergence signal, the divergence is most likely valid.

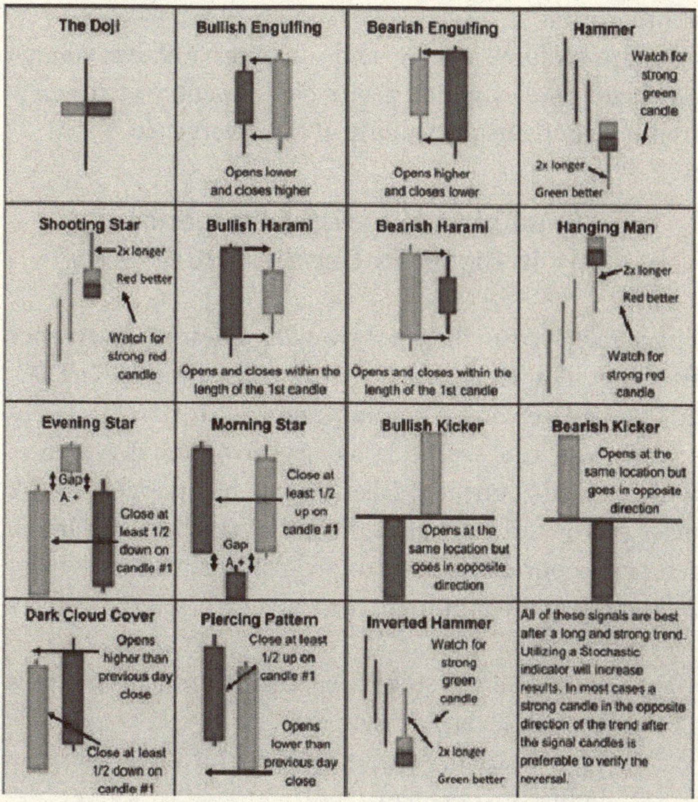

Confirm the Validity Using Volume

Volume shift may also confirm the divergence. In a downtrend, the price is falling down on high volume. But after divergence, the volume dries up, because now the price movement is against the trend (for the time being). If the volume dries up, it is a signal that traders are being cautious and not entering the new trend, but waiting for confirmation.

If the volume picks up and you observe higher volume on those candles which are in the direction of the new trend, it confirms the validity of the divergence.

Example of Bearish Divergence in Close-By Candles: HUL

I have retrieved an old chart showing a bearish divergence from my files. Here, a divergence takes place on Oct. 23, 2014 on a Deepavali Muhurat trading chart.

As you can see, it is a very powerful divergence, with a signal count of 3 (that means the divergence took place on the third day after the initial top/bottom). If you remember our discussion from Chapter 3, you know that 3 candles are the minimum for a divergence.

- First bullish, second bearish, third bullish (in a bearish divergence).
- First bearish, second bullish, third bearish (in a bullish divergence).

Thereafter, the stock market was closed from Oct. 24–26 due to the weekend and holidays.

Below, you can see the chart of the next day (it is a daily chart, but you will still get a rough idea of how quickly divergence gave its results).

HUL fell 5% on flat results (the second-last candle is of Oct. 27 on a daily chart).

Here, we get the idea that RSI signals from a smaller timeframe can also give good results for larger timeframes.

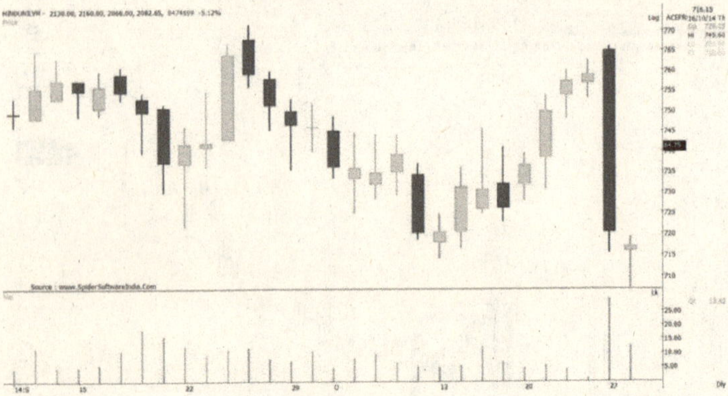

Example of Bearish Divergence in Far-Off Candles: Nifty 60-Minute

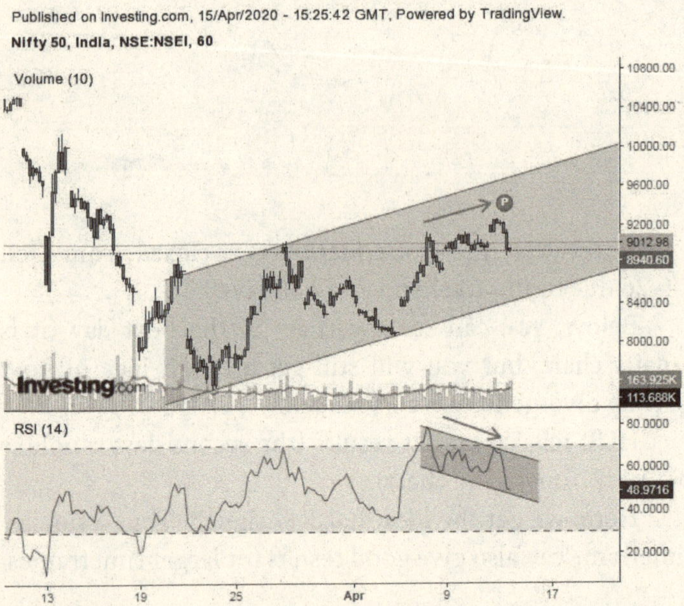

As Paul Dean says, positive divergences lead to negative reversals; negative divergences lead to positive reversals.

That means divergences lead to reversals.

So what should we do next?

We should move on to another powerful RSI signal: **reversals.**

CHAPTER 6

Reversals: Positive and Negative

"If you pick up only a single notion from this book. let it be the following: When an oscillator advances or declines disproportionately to the markets' movement, you are on the wrong side of the market if you are positioned with the oscillator."

— Constance Brown

As I have already said, positive and negative reversals were not invented by Welles Wilder, but are Andrew Cardwell's contribution to the RSI.

Welles Wilder moved on to other things, but Cardwell stuck with the RSI, and in doing so discovered reversals. Some people also name them 'hidden divergences', which is a highly confusing term that adds complexity to the already complex world of the RSI.

Key Differences Between Divergences and Reversals

Remember, reversals are different from divergences; in fact, they are just the opposite.

	Divergences	**Reversals**
Trend	Divergences signify trend reversals.	Reversals signify trend continuation.
Measurement during downtrend	Divergence is measured off of the lows of *the price and the indicator* during a downtrend.	Negative reversal is measured off of the highs of *the price and the indicator* during a downtrend.
Measurement during uptrend	Divergence is measured off of the highs of *the price and the indicator* during an uptrend.	Positive reversal is measured off of the lows of *the price and the indicator* during an uptrend.
Placement	At the extreme range of the price chart AND near overbought/oversold levels of the RSI.	Reversals are found mostly in the middle range of the panel.

- The trendline for positive reversals is drawn at the bottom/support line of the price and RSI charts (just like we do in a bullish divergence).
- The trendline for negative reversals is drawn at the top/resistance line of the price and RSI charts (just like we do in a bearish divergence).

As Paul Dean puts it, divergences are usually the 'signs', whereas reversals are usually the 'signals'.

He means that you can trade on a reversal signal, whereas you can't trade on a divergence signal by setting a price objective.

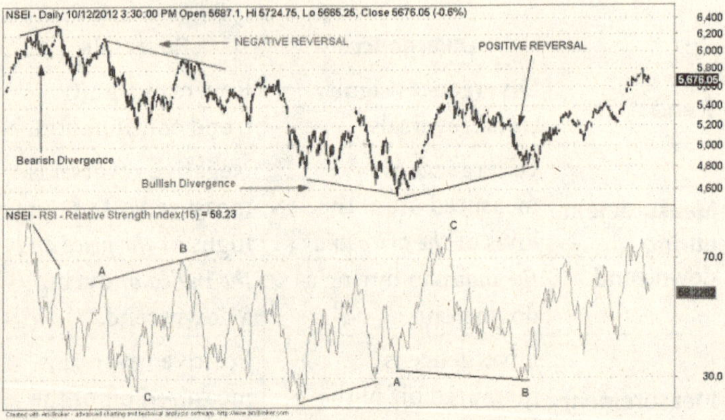

Positive Reversals and Negative Reversals

A positive reversal occurs:

When the price makes a higher low while the RSI makes a lower low.

The price proceeds to rise.

- Positive reversals only occur in bullish trends.
- Positive reversal trendlines are drawn on lows.

A negative reversal occurs:

When the price makes a lower high while the RSI makes a higher high.

The price proceeds to fall.

- Negative reversals only occur in bearish trends.
- Negative reversal trendlines are drawn on highs.

	Positive reversal	Negative reversal
Trend	In uptrends	In downtrends
Trend continuation	Signals continuation of an uptrend	Signals continuation of a downtrend
Retracement pattern	Occurs in uptrend retracements	Occurs in downtrend retracements
Price/RSI lows	The price makes higher lows, the RSI makes lower lows	The price makes lower highs, the RSI makes higher highs
Measurement	Measured off of the lows of the price and the indicator	Measured off of the highs of the price and the indicator
Placement	In the middle of the price chart	In the middle of the price chart

Positive Reversals

Positive reversals are seen during uptrends. They occur at the time of corrections or retracements, when the stock falls due to normal profit booking of traders and not due to serious sell-off.

As the stock is running in a strong uptrend, its up average for the past 14 days is significantly high. When there is a reverse movement in the price, the RSI reacts strongly and falls disproportionately.

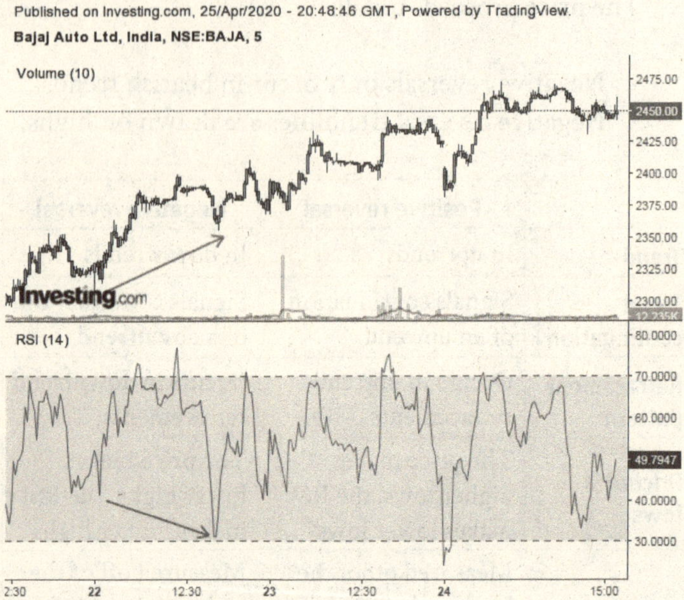

As we have seen in our discussion in Chapter 3, the RSI moves disproportionately on anti-trend prices. So the RSI falls down more than it should, and creates a positive reversal in the process.

After retracement, new buyers come in, and even those who have booked profit join in, as they once again find the stock price attractive. The momentum builds up and the uptrend continues.

Negative Reversals

Negative reversals come during downtrends. The stock is falling down, and the RSI is also falling down with it.

Suddenly, short sellers book profits and there is short

covering. The price moves up slightly, but the RSI moves up sharply on this anti-trend price action.

In this process, it creates a negative reversal.

After retracement, new short sellers join, or the old short sellers rejoin the party, and due to this, the downtrend continues.

Important Tip

Spike lows of the RSI are observed in an uptrend, and spike highs of the RSI are observed in a downtrend.

How To Calculate the Price Target

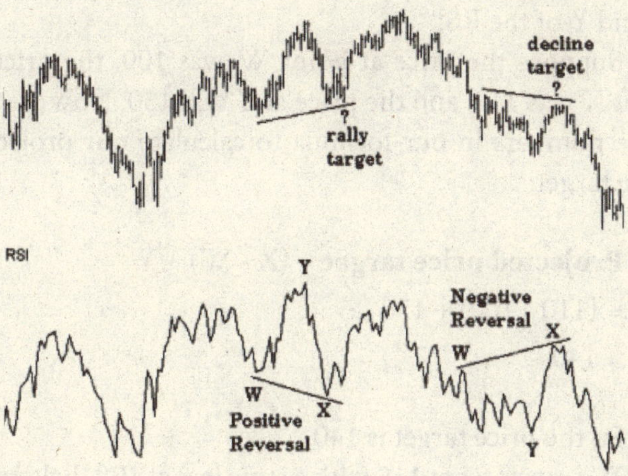

Positive and negative reversals are preferred by traders, as they allow you to set targets and stop-losses, which is difficult in the case of a divergence. Here, you know where to enter and where to place your stop-loss.

Good traders want to determine the risk-reward ratio in advance. And to know this ratio, they have to know their entry price, stop-loss, and target price.

Price Target Formula for a Positive Reversal Signal

Price Target = (X - W) + Y

Note: Don't get confused into thinking that X is lower than W (I was also confused by this at first). You are looking at the wrong panel. See the price panel, where the price at X is higher than the price at W, So the formula is alright. You just have to find out what the price was at W, X, and Y of the RSI.

Suppose the price at point W was 100, the price at point X was 110, and the price at Y was 130. Now we put these numbers in our formula to calculate our projected price target:

Projected price target = (X - W) + Y

= (110 - 100) + 130

= 140

So the price target is 140.

We can enter at 115 with a stop-loss at 109 (below the recent low of 110).

If we do so, here is our trade setup:

- Risk = Rs. 7
- Reward = Rs. 25
- Risk-reward ratio = 25:7 = 3.6:1

Not bad!

Price Target Formula for a Negative Reversal Signal

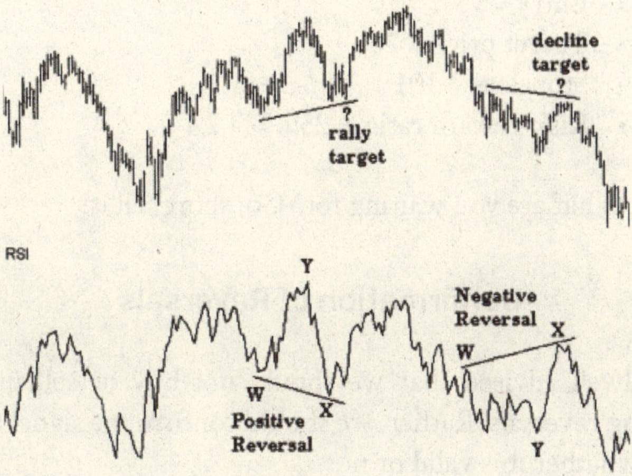

Suppose, in a negative reversal, the price at point W was 110, the price at X was 100, and the price at Y was 80. Now we put these numbers in our formula to calculate our projected price target:

Projected price target = Y - (W - X)

= 80 - (110- 100)

= 70

So the projected price target is 70.

Here, also, you can determine your stop-loss—maybe at 101—one rupee more than X.

And then it is easy to calculate your risk-reward ratio.

Suppose you enter at 95 (at least that much of a margin has to be left because pattern recognition takes time, there are ask-bid spreads, and there are commissions, brokerages, etc. too).

- Entry = 95
- Target price = 70
- Stop-loss = 101
- Risk-reward ratio = 25:6 = 4.2:1

What are you waiting for? Go; short sell it.

Confirmation of Reversals

Cardwell advised that we should not buy or sell upon seeing reversals. Rather, we should confirm the signal and see whether it is valid or not.

His recommendation is to get confirmation from the moving averages of the RSI (not of the price).

- Confirmation of positive reversal—the 9 SMA and WMA of the RSI should point upwards.
- Confirmation of negative reversal—the 9 SMA and 45 WMA of the RSI should point downwards.

Cancellation: If the divergence trendline is broken, it cancels out the divergence.

When you get the opposite signal, you book profits and exit. As Paul Dean says, "The Positive Reversal is over as soon as the NR is confirmed. What do we do? Exit. Simple."

Reversals Are Trend Continuation Signals

Reversal patterns are primarily useful for trend traders, as the occurrence of this pattern signals that prices have made a corrective retracement in a larger trend—and that the trend is ready to resume.

The main benefit of trading with a reversal pattern is that the majority of the market's momentum is on your side, as you are trading in the same direction as the larger trend.

This is a key difference between the reversal pattern and the classic divergence, and one that many new traders miss when looking to implement these strategies. The occurrence of a reversal pattern can also act as a confirmation that the original trend is still valid.

Close-By Reference Points Are More Powerful

Cardwell prefers close-by reference points for his reversal patterns. That means that they should ideally be separated by a single price bar. Such signals, which are separated by one or two bars, are 'strong' signals, as they ensure that projected targets are achieved.

For example, let us talk about positive reversals. Say a stock makes a low at 85 (W). The next day, it gives a green candle at 90 (Y). On the third day, it makes a red candle at 88 (X). What would be the projected target?

Remember the formula for positive reversals:

Projected price target = (X - W) + Y

= (88 - 85) + 90

= 93

Can you see the problem here?

Try putting a stop-loss and try to calculate the risk-reward ratio.

Now perhaps you might see the problem—the profit margin is too low.

So why did Cardwell advocate for this so strongly?

The key is in the details.

Perhaps Cardwell laid down this rule for forex markets, where low profit margins are considered the norm.

But the real reason is this: we are thinking in terms of daily charts, but Cardwell preferred weekly charts, and we all know that a weekly candle is necessarily bigger.

Cardwell's insistence on close-by reference points can only be understood in terms of weekly or monthly charts.

Say that on a weekly chart, a stock makes a low at 85 (W). The next day, it gives a green candle at 125 (Y). On the third day, it makes a red candle at 90 (X). What would be the projected target?

Projected price target = (X - W) + Y

= (90 - 85) + 125

= 130

Now the risk-reward ratio, stop-loss, and projected price target all fall in line.

So here we conclude our discussion of the top 10 signals of the RSI, which we started in Chapter 4.

In the next chapter, we will look at the limitations of the RSI. It can create magic, yet that does not mean that it can create magic all the time, at all places, in all markets, and for all stocks.

Up until now, we have learnt when we should use the RSI; now, we will learn when not to use the RSI.

CHAPTER 7

Limitations of the RSI

"Markets tend to operate in a trading range 70–75% of the time and trend 25–30% of the time. Consequently, any moving average time period should be equally effective in a trending market and no moving average is effective in a trading range market. Conversely, oscillators that identify areas of overbought and oversold are most effective in trading range or sideways markets."

— **Thomas DeMark**

The RSI is a dynamic indicator that goes beyond its functions as a momentum oscillator. However, like any other indicator, it has its own limitations.

You have to be aware of these limitations so that you don't use the RSI where it can't or shouldn't be used.

- First of all, the RSI is a momentum oscillator, so it does not work well in trends—or so people say. This is the general consensus about the RSI. However, as we have seen, divergences and reversals can also work well during trends. So this 'limitation' is not 100% correct.

- It does not work well in illiquid or low-float scrips, so don't try to trade low-float or low-volume stocks on the basis of the RSI. The reason is simple: small quantities of buy or sell orders can swing prices disproportionately. Look for a stock with good volume—preferably above 1 lakh shares daily.
- It does not work well in operator-driven stocks or circuit stocks.
- It does not work properly in a stock with very high volatility; in such cases, the RSI may give inconsistent signals.
- Theoretically, it does not work well in index charts, though it works like a charm in the Nifty chart. The theory is that an index is a sum of several stocks, so the cumulative movement may not give consistent readings. However, practically speaking, I have seen it working well on the Nifty 50 index.
- It is calculated only on the basis of closing prices, so day highs or day lows will not be counted, even if such price movements are significant.
- It may give false or disproportionate signals, especially in anti-trend directions. Even small anti-trend price action can cause major movement in the RSI.
- As we have already discussed in Chapter 1, different websites give different RSI readings, so ensure that your reading is correct. For the purposes of this book, always consult Investing.com, a free online charting website, for RSI readings.
- Day traders prefer to use short periods on the RSI; some use even 3- or 2-period RSI to generate

more signals.

- Use of the RSI is very subjective. The trader's experience plays a crucial role.
- In a nutshell, the RSI gives us a snapshot of the bear-bull power balance. Whenever there is a momentum shift due to some significant news, the RSI alerts us about it before the price action does. It is very sensitive to any changes in momentum. Other indicators need signal lines or the support of multiple moving averages, but a single RSI line is capable of doing all that work—and doing it better.
- If someone tells you trading is simple, don't believe him. He is either kidding or has the mentality of a child. The stock market is full of jolly-hearted professionals whose mission in life is to make the life of retail traders difficult and teach them some lessons in the bargain. They use shakeouts and fakeouts with the RSI, too, just like your centre forward does in hockey: feigning and pretending to do one thing, while actually planning on doing something else.
- The most popular feigning trick used by professionals is this: when they want to give a breakout, they just pause the buying pressure. The RSI is very volatile around 70, so even with a slight decrease, it falls below 70, causing retail traders to think that the RSI is reversing and the price is going to fall down. So some of them sell, or even short sell, the stock. Then the laughing professionals put the pressure on the buy pedal and kill the short sellers by staging a breakout.

CHAPTER 8

Which Timeframe Is Best?

"Well, I use 14-period on a monthly, weekly, daily, hourly, 15-minute chart, 5-minute chart. The rules don't change depending on the temperament and investment objective of a trader."

— Andrew Cardwell

There are so many timeframes that you get different RSI signals regarding buy, sell, or hold. (I wonder if anyone ever got an RSI signal of HOLD?)

In Chapter 1, we had talked about several challenges associated with RSI trading; one of the major challenges is regarding timeframes.

The Challenge of Deciding the Chart Timeframe

Look at the various timeframe chart options available on Investing.com:

- 1-minute chart
- 5-minute chart
- 15-minute chart
- 30-minute chart
- 45-minute chart
- 1-hour chart
- 2-hour chart
- 4-hour chart
- 5-hour chart
- 1-day chart
- 1-week chart
- 1-month chart

Interesting Note: Spider Software provides a still higher timeframe chart option: 3-month chart (quarterly chart).

When there are 12 different timeframe charts, there will naturally be 12 different RSI levels of a single stock or index at any point in time.

I will show you an example after the market close on 5.5.2020:

Timeframe	RSI Level
1-minute chart	56.25
5-minute chart	30.23
15-minute chart	32.12
30-minute chart	28.35
45-minute chart	33.10
1-hour chart	34.56

2-hour chart	41.72
4-hour chart	48.15
5-hour chart	48.08
1-day chart	48.51
1-week chart	36.89
1-month chart	39.53
Average RSI	39.79

Now let us briefly discuss what the different RSI levels tell us.

- The 1-minute chart has the highest RSI reading. It means that in the last 14 minutes, buy momentum was stronger than sell momentum. Other minute charts are showing lesser RSI readings, so we may conclude that it was a down day, and so the 1-minute chart is showing short covering and intraday settlement or profit booking.
- Five of these charts, from the 5-minute chart to the 1-hour chart, show the RSI around level 30. It means that there, the RSI is near oversold levels and the current trend is likely to be down. The minute charts' low readings also tell us that it was a down day.
- Three of these charts (4-hour, 5-hour and 1-day) are showing the RSI around level 48; this means that the buy and sell equation is almost in equilibrium. It indicates that over the past two weeks, momentum has been uncertain and there may be some indecision about the direction.

Interesting Note

By the way, do you know anybody who trades on the basis of 2-hour, 4-hour, or 5-hour charts? I didn't even know they existed.

The weekly RSI is at 37 and the monthly RSI is at 39.

The weekly RSI is less than the daily RSI, which means that the market has crashed within the previous 14 weeks.

Which Timeframe Is Best?

Remember, the price levels remain unchanged across all timeframes, but the RSI levels change in different timeframes. And this is the root of a lot of confusion.

Why?

Because the RSI is calculated on the closing price of a bar. In a 1-minute chart, the RSI changes every minute because the price makes a new candle every minute and the RSI is calculated every minute. In a 1-day chart, it changes every day because the price makes a new candle every day. So the RSI gives different readings across different timeframes.

These different timeframes pose a unique challenge for traders: which timeframe is best?

Well, it depends! It depends on your psychology, your capital, your holding capacity, your profit expectations, and whether you have the luxury of sitting in front of your computer during market hours for day trading. If you trade only on a part-time basis and you have some other full-time job or profession, day trading is obviously not a viable option for you. So you can conveniently forget about minute charts.

Though there are several opinions on the subject, this is the overall consensus:

- **For day trading:** 5-minute chart, 15-minute chart
- **For swing/positional trading:** 1-hour chart
- **For short-term trading (less than a year):** Daily chart
- **For long-term trading (more than a year):** Weekly chart

One Level Up, One Level Down

Always consult the charts of one level up and one level down.

What does that mean? It means that if you are trading on the basis of daily charts, you should also look at one level up (in this case, weekly) and one level down (1-hour charts) to filter the noise and get a proper perspective.

- **Focus:** Daily chart
- **One level up:** Weekly chart
- **One level down:** 1-hour chart

You may ask why we shouldn't choose a 5-hour chart for one level down. Your query is valid, but the answer is obvious. Theoretically speaking, the 5-hour chart is the next timeframe, but virtually nobody trades on the basis of

2-hour, 4-hour, or 5-hour charts. So the next logical down level is the 1-hour chart.

Most traders only use 1-minute, 5-minute, 15-minute, 1-hour, 1-day, and 1-week charts. So though there are theoretically 12 timeframes available on Investing.com, there are practically only 6 timeframes to choose from:

- 1-minute chart
- 5-minute chart
- 15-minute chart
- 1-hour chart
- 1-day chart
- 1-week chart

If you follow this strategy of one level up and one level down, you will be better off. This gives you the advantage of seeing the price action through various viewpoints. It may also alert you to some red flag that might be present in a lower or higher timeframe, but not in your timeframe.

Remember the one step up and one step down formula, and consult the charts of timeframes one step higher and one step lower.

What is the advantage of consulting lower timeframe charts? You will get to see earlier signals. A potential trend reversal is seen first in smaller timeframes.

What is the advantage of consulting higher timeframe charts? You will get to see the context or background. You will also get the idea of the broader trend of your stock or index.

Some people say that the RSI was invented for daily charts, so the RSI works best in that timeframe. However,

Andrew Cardwell has shown that it can work equally well in a weekly timeframe as well. But let us not forget that Cardwell had modified the RSI to suit his purposes. If we want to trade a different timeframe other than daily, we can also do so. Remember, lower timeframe chart signals would give less profit percentage compared to higher timeframes. So don't expect to find a 20% profit projection signal on a 1-minute chart. Be realistic and expect only a 2% profit signal on a 1-minute chart.

If you want a higher profit percentage, trade on the basis of higher timeframe charts. Though there is a catch: while higher timeframes promise better profits, the drawback is that you will have to wait longer to collect your profits. The higher the profit percentage you require, the higher the timeframe you should choose, but be ready to wait for a longer time to book your profits.

The Challenge of Deciding the Number of Periods in the RSI

Most day traders reduce the number of periods (*n*) on the RSI to generate more signals. Reducing the number of periods makes the RSI more volatile (where you get more signals), and increasing the number of periods makes the RSI more stable (where you get less signals). Some day traders use a 9-period RSI, and some even use a 3- or 2-period RSI.

However, there are some experts who strongly advise that 14 periods should always be used for the RSI in all time horizons due to its peculiar predictive capacity. They say that only a 14-period RSI works effectively as a leading indicator. In other timeframes, it somehow, somewhat loses its predictive power.

The Challenge of Deciding the Trend

Let us not forget that when we shift our timeframe, the trend also shifts.

When you are looking at different timeframe charts, you should know what the dominant trend is. It is quite possible to find an uptrend in a weekly chart, a downtrend in a daily chart, and an uptrend in an hourly chart.

Now what do you do? Which trend should you go with?

Deciding the trend is a crucial question for traders, as major price action happens with the trend. As the saying goes, "the trend is your friend".

You simply write down:

- **Weekly:** Up
- **Daily:** Down
- **Hourly:** Up

Of course, the higher-timeframe chart determines the long-term trend of the stock, but other timeframes play their roles in determining intermediate and short-term trends.

In our example, the weekly chart is in a primary uptrend. But its short-term trend is down—maybe due to profit booking, retracement, newsflow, or whatever. This is why you are observing a downtrend in the daily chart.

You should do well to remember that the daily chart

is in a downtrend because a retracement is taking place in the weekly chart.

As soon as the weekly chart's retracement is over, you will see a shift in the daily chart trend, and it will start a new uptrend. Perhaps around this time, you will see a bullish divergence on the daily chart, which would alert you that the trend is going to change. It will foretell that now, the daily chart is going to move in sync with the weekly chart's primary trend.

Larger-timeframe charts determine long-term trends, while shorter-timeframe charts often give early signals about trend changes.

In a nutshell, this sums up the whole thing:

Timeframe	Primary Trend	Secondary Trend
Weekly Chart	Up	Down
Daily Chart	Down	Up
Hourly Chart	Up	

You can see that the secondary trend of the higher timeframe may become the primary trend of the lower timeframe.

Always get some clarity on trends in different timeframes, as it will save you a lot of confusion. When you look at three different timeframe charts, you may see conflicting signals on them. You may see a sell signal on the daily chart, but a buy signal on the hourly chart.

Usually, we should trade in the direction of the one-step-higher timeframe, so we can do one of these two things:

- Wait for those signals which are in sync with the higher timeframe's trend
- Enter anyway with a tight stop-loss.

Why the Timeframe Is Important

Choosing the right timeframe is important because traders of every timeframe have distinct personalities.

If you trade a 5-minute chart, you will think like those traders who also trade on the basis of 5-minute charts.

You won't care for a long-term approach, you will adhere to a tight stop-loss, you will look out for pennies, and you will book profits quickly. Their motto is: in quick, out quick. They usually don't have much money or patience.

Nothing wrong with that! However, this is the typical personality of this particular timeframe, and if you are trading on the basis of 5-minute charts, you have to adopt this philosophy. A 5-minute chart trader is not bothered about long-term profits or losses; he is not bothered whether a company is going to go bankrupt tomorrow. He is concerned only with here and now. This is why he will often take more risky trades.

Minute chart traders usually trade futures and options, as they have better profit potential there. They lack a solid capital base, so they frequently trade on margins. You see, if you don't have much capital, you can't buy and hold stocks. You have to necessarily trade in the F&O segment. However, don't forget that even big institutions—FIIs and DIIs—trade in the F&O segment. They have a lot of capital at their disposal. For any retail trader, getting profits in

F&O is akin to David fighting Goliath.

On the other hand, typical daily chart traders are usually retail investors who have some full-time job or profession and invest their residual or disposable income with a months-long trading timeframe. Some of them can't track the market during market hours. They are not in a hurry to book profits and they have more money than day traders. They don't consult minute charts and they are not bothered about short-term hiccups. They want higher profit percentages than day traders. Some of them are swing traders; some of them are SIP investors. Most are part-time traders who are investing their hard-earned money in the stock market to earn a better yield than a bank FD would provide. They are conservative and safety-oriented.

Those who trade on the basis of weekly charts are in a different class. Usually, the opinion of the larger-timeframe traders prevails, as they have more money, more patience, and more power to move the markets for a longer period. Usually, large timeframe investors are mutual funds, pension funds, big financial institutions, FIIs, or big traders/investors. They typically have a longer timeframe; for short-term profits, they trade in the F&O segment. Remember, they are the experts with top degrees in finance. And due to their clout, they often have access to insider news much earlier than retail traders.

Important Tip

Daily charts are mostly used by retail investors, and weekly charts are mostly used by institutional investors (though they sometimes also pay attention to monthly charts, as they invest for a longer period).

No wonder retail shareholders and professionals don't seem to be on the same page! You see, they take decisions on the basis of different charts. So if you intend to trade like a pro, start paying attention to those charts which professionals see. In particular, study weekly charts well, as it is the favourite timeframe of big investors.

The Challenge of Multiple Overbought/Oversold Levels

Different timeframes can create some confusion in the case of the RSI.

Suppose you are a trader whose primary chart is the daily chart.

You check the one-level-down chart, and in the 1-hour chart, you find that the RSI is above 70, which means it is overbought. Instantly, you think: is it going to fall from here?

You check the daily chart; there, you find that the RSI is at level 60 and has plenty of space to move up.

And if you go one level up and check the weekly

chart, you find that the RSI is at level 50, so it is practically starting its upmove after crossing the centreline.

Higher timeframe signals will prevail, but the RSI will find a way to manage the whole thing. You see, in a strong uptrend, even a single red candle would bring the 1-hour RSI from level 70 to 30. Have faith in the RSI, and whenever you see overbought levels in a lower timeframe chart, be prepared to see a short period of correction.

Important Tip

If the weekly trend is up and the daily trend shows signs of weakness, it may be a time of retracement in the weekly trend. So you can improve your timing if you use a lower-timeframe chart to tell you the retracements of the higher timeframe.

CHAPTER 9

20 Popular RSI Trading Strategies

"At best you may achieve a 60% win rate with any strategy, including one with the RSI."

— Tradingsim.com

There are, in fact, scores of different ways to trade with the RSI. In this chapter, you will find 20 popular trading strategies where traders use the RSI to their advantage, either independently or with the help of some other tool/ indicator.

Look at them, check them out, and, if you find any appealing, backtest them and update your arsenal of trading strategies.

The RSI alone is a mighty force, but it has so many facets, meaning we can easily misunderstand its message. I am often so preoccupied with divergences that due to my focus on them, I miss noticing reversals till it is too late.

This is why it is necessary to confirm RSI signals by using other indicators or signals—though, frankly speaking, I don't think that moving averages can help here. As we have already discussed, moving averages are lagging indicators, while the RSI is a leading indicator. However, these eight confirmation tools are generally used in RSI trading:

1. Price trendlines and RSI trendlines (for finding support and resistance levels)
2. Horizontal support and resistance levels (because price has a memory)
3. Bollinger Bands
4. Moving average crossover
5. Moving averages of the RSI itself
6. Bullish or bearish candles at critical junctures
7. Higher timeframe charts
8. Volume

"Volume tends to build when prices move in their primary direction; it tends to fall during the counter-trend, during corrections or during pauses in a stock's move."

— Donald L. Cassidy

Remember: today, most trading is done by computers with algorithms by big brokers, banks, or big traders. So we have to prepare a solid strategy.

Important Tip

Most retail traders want a 100% success rate, which is impossible in the stock market. This is why they don't set a stop-loss or book losses, but hang on to the losers. They don't have a trading strategy in place; hope is their strategy.

In my opinion, traders should aim for a 50% success rate. Be prepared to be wrong 5 times out of 10 when making trades. Naturally, this should compel you to devise a better strategy where you let your winners run and cut short the losers. I plead guilty here, too; I should also remember this.

If you don't believe me, at least listen to Andrew Cardwell's advice: "We're a trader. We go to the market, and we know we're going to try and make profits, we're going to take losses, but you have to be willing to admit when you're wrong because the most successful traders in the world are only right 30% to 40% of the time just like batting title. You're not going to hit a home run every time. You don't try and hit a home run. Try and understand what the market is showing you."

So here are 20 popular RSI trading strategies to give you an idea of how some traders utilize the RSI:

1. RSI + Support/Resistance Level

- The 14-period RSI is below 30 (oversold).
- The price is testing a support zone.

- Buy above any bullish price candle/bar.

2. Vanilla RSI

This is the simplest of strategies. That is why it is called a vanilla strategy.

- Buy when the RSI crosses the 30 level from below.
- Exit when the RSI reaches near the 70 level.

3. 2-Period RSI

The 2-period RSI is the brainchild of Larry Connors. This unconventional lookback period turns the RSI into an incredible short-term timing tool.

Traders should look for buying opportunities when the 2-period RSI moves below 10.

First, identify the major trend using a long-term moving average; Connors recommends a 200-day moving average. The long-term trend is up when a security is above its 200-day SMA.

Traders should look for buying opportunities when above the 200-day SMA.

Connors advocates exiting long positions on a move above the 5-day SMA.

4. Centreline Crossover

Previously, we have seen the vanilla RSI. This is somewhat similar, as it is so basic.

- Whenever the RSI crosses the centreline of 50 from below, go long.
- When it nears the 70 level, exit.

5. RSI Double Bottom

This strategy is based partly on Wilder's failure swing concept (W pattern) and partly on bullish divergences. It improves the odds of success, though there is no guarantee that the RSI will not ditch you in between.

The first price bottom is made on heavy volume. After the first price sell-off, which also results in a breach of 30 on the RSI, the stock will have a snapback rally.

This rally is short-lived and is then followed by another snapback reaction which breaks the low of the first bottom.

This second low is where stops are run from the first reaction low. Shortly after breaking the low by a few ticks, the security begins to rally sharply. This second low forms a double bottom not only on the price chart but on the relative strength index as well.

The reason this second rally has legs is: (1) the weak longs were stopped out of their position on the second reaction, and (2) the new shorts are being squeezed out of their position. The combination of these two forces produces sharp rallies in a very short timeframe.

6. Price/RSI Divergence

This is a simple and solid strategy, though there are several ifs and buts here.

- Buy when you find a bullish divergence of the RSI—when the price makes a fresh low, but the RSI does not.
- Sell at bearish price action or at the resistance level.

As we discussed in Chapter 5 (on divergences), the RSI tends to give multiple divergences, so if you buy on the first divergence itself, the price may not support your decision. Usually, it is safer to buy on the second divergence.

7. RSI Inverted Head and Shoulders

- Buy when you see an inverted head and shoulders (a bullish trend reversal signal) on the RSI panel.
- Book profits when the RSI nears 70.
- For confirmation, buy on a bullish candle and on a support.

8. RSI Resistance Trendline Breakout

When the RSI breaks its own resistance trendline, it is time to go long.

It is usually safe, but we should seek confirmation from candles and support as well as resistance levels. Volume can also confirm the RSI breakout.

9. RSI Trendline Support

- Buy when the RSI takes support at its own support line and starts moving up.

- Close the position when the RSI nears 70.

10. RSI + Bullish Engulfing

- Buy when the RSI gives an oversold signal and leaves the zone, AND a bullish engulfing candle appears on the chart.
- Close the position when the RSI nears 70.

11. RSI + MACD

- Buy when the RSI gives a oversold signal, which is supported by a MACD signal line crossing.
- Close the position if either indicator provides an exit signal.

12. Positive Reversal

- In an uptrend, buy when you see a positive reversal after which the price starts moving up.
- Calculate the profit by the formula provided in Chapter 6 (on reversals).
- Close the position slightly below the projected target.

13. RSI + Price Channel

This strategy can only be adopted in price channels.

- Buy when the price bounces from the bottom line of the channel and the RSI bounces from its oversold zone.
- Close your position when the price nears the upper line of the channel.

14. RSI + Moving Averages

This is used by forex day traders.

- **Timeframe:** 1 day
- **Moving averages:** 5-period EMA and 12-period EMA

Buy when the 5-period EMA crosses the 12-period EMA from below to the upside AND the RSI is above level 50.

15. RSI + Bollinger Bands

Day traders use this strategy in 1-minute charts.

- **Bollinger Band period:** 40
- **RSI period:** 6

Buy when the price rises from the lower line of the Bollinger Band and the RSI increases from level 20.

The traditional way of using Bollinger Bands is to trade for reversals. If a price hits the upper or lower band, it is likely to reverse, as prices have already reached the extreme end.

Confirmations:

- RSI divergence
- Bullish candlestick patterns

If you are looking to buy, the ideal time would be when the price is at the lower band, the RSI is oversold, there is a bullish RSI divergence, and the candlestick shows a bullish pattern.

16. RSI + Moving Averages

This strategy is for day trading. It is an RSI/MA crossover entry strategy. It is a low-profit, low-risk strategy.

In an hourly (60-minute chart) chart, set the RSI to 21 periods.

Get a 10-period moving average of the RSI.

Trades are only taken in the direction of the trend, so wait for an uptrend to buy.

- During an uptrend, the RSI moves below 40.
- After that, when the RSI crosses back its own moving average (10), go long.
- Close your position when the price moves a little in your favour.

17. RSI + 20 SMA

This is a swing trading strategy which uses daily charts.

RSI period: 5 days.

- The price has to be above the 20 SMA, indicating an uptrend.
- Wait for the price to pull down to touch the 20 SMA line.
- Now look at the RSI—see if it has bottomed below the 50 level and started to turn up.
- This is the buy signal. Take quick profits.

18. 9-day RSI Average Crossover

Here, the signal line of a 9-day exponential RSI average is used, about which we have already talked.

- Buy when the RSI line crosses its average line from below to the upside.
- Close your position after a little profit.

19. RSI + Stochastic + MA

MA: 10 periods

Buy when:

- The price is crossing the MA from below to up.
- The RSI and stochastic exit oversold zone.

All three signals should be received within three candles; otherwise, they will lose their value.

20. RSI + CCI

RSI period: 30
CCI period: 6

- Buy when the RSI is above the 50 line and the CCI gives -100 crossovers from below.
- Close your position when the RSI crosses the 50 line from above to below.

CHAPTER 10

Busting the Myth: Can the RSI Remain Oversold/Overbought for Several Months?

Experts say that a stock can remain in an oversold or overbought zone for several months, or even years.

Well, that's a myth; it doesn't happen on daily charts.

In my studies of daily charts of the Nifty index, I didn't find it to be true. I didn't find a single stock which has remained oversold or overbought for more than three months on the daily charts.

- Maybe such a thing happens in forex or commodities.
- Or maybe it happens in operator-driven stocks or circuit stocks like Ruchi Soya.
- Or maybe it happens in higher-timeframe charts than daily charts.

In my studies of the Nifty 50 stocks for the past 15 years, I found that on WEEKLY charts, Brittania, Bajaj Auto, GAIL, Grasim, HDFC, HDFC Bank, Hero Moto,

HUL, ICICI Bank, Infosys, IOC, ITC, L&T, Mahindra & Mahindra, Maruti, Nestle, Reliance, Shree Cement, TCS, Titan, Vedanta, etc. remained in the overbought zone for more than 4–6 months at a time.

However, during the same period, the RSI didn't remain overbought on their daily charts.

For example, check the WEEKLY chart of Brittania, in which the RSI remained in the overbought zone for 10 months:

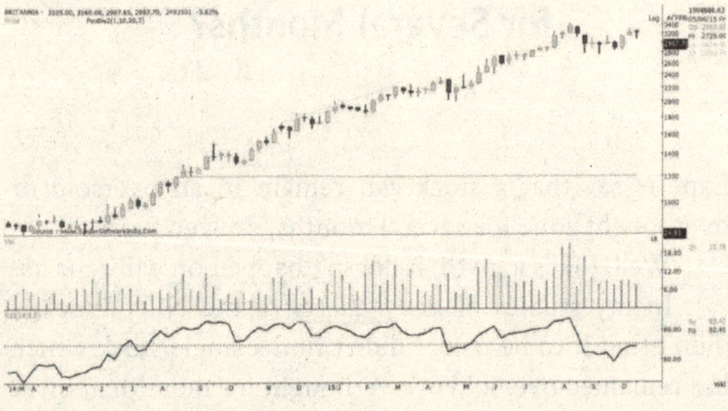

However, on the daily chart, it was not in the overbought zone for so long. It kept on crossing the 70 line quite frequently both ways.

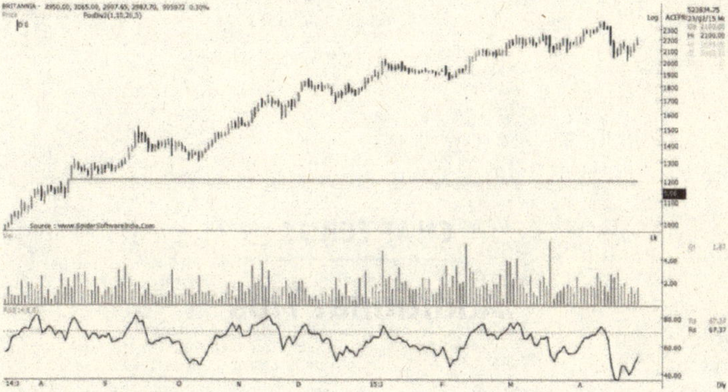

And there was no chart, weekly or daily, where the RSI remained in the oversold zone for more than 4 months.

So, as you can see, it was a myth we only believed because we relied on the experts, who told us about overextended durations, but didn't tell us that they only happen in terms of WEEKLY charts—and rarely, at that.

In my studies of 50 Nifty stocks, I found that it has only happened once or at most twice in the last 15 years. And it only happened in 40% stock charts. So it is quite a rare sight! But yes, it can happen in weekly charts. You see, four months means 18 candles, and it might happen when the atmosphere is quite bullish. But four months means 90 candles or so in a daily chart, so it is not likely to happen. Why? Because even a small anti-trend movement in the price is enough to eject the RSI from the overbought zone.

In longer timeframes, the RSI can remain in overbought for months (for weekly charts) or years (in monthly charts), but it happens rarely even then.

CHAPTER 11

Additional Tips

"I've always used three keys to success I talk to people about when I give a presentation—methodology, patience, and discipline. The discipline to follow your rules, stay within your rules, control your emotions; and the patience to, as I quote, say allow the market to show you what it wants to do, not what you want it to do. Well, a lot of people force the issue. Nobody holds a gun to my head to tell me what to trade."

— Andrew Cardwell

- Usually, levels 60–70 on the RSI are considered overbought, but during breakouts, the RSI in a 60–70 range is considered the best.
- The RSI shows the relative strength of a stock as compared to that stock's historical strength. If the RSI is above 60, it means that a stock is strong and it is in a good position to give a powerful breakout. A breakout needs a lot of power, and if a stock is weak, either the breakout would be unsuccessful or it would not prove very profitable. The RSI's best level at the time of a breakout should be more than

60 and less than 70. Why? Why doesn't the RSI give breakouts more often above level 70? Why do breakouts take place when the RSI is generally between levels 50–70? There is a simple reason behind this. If the RSI reaches its overbought level of 70, investors and short sellers would increase the supply of the stock by selling it. Bulls don't want significant supply of the stock at the time of a breakout, which is sure to come if the RSI reaches 70, so they seize the opportunity when the RSI is below 70, so that additional supply doesn't upset their breakout plans.

- In my studies of descending channel breakouts, I found that 75% of the breakouts occurred when the RSI was in the range of 51–70. Whenever you are in a dilemma whether a stock may give a breakout or not, look at the RSI levels. If the RSI is between 51–70, study the possibility seriously; otherwise, don't bother. You may miss 25% of your chances, but you will still be able to make quick decisions about the other 75% that come your way.
- RSI divergence is the key to channel breakouts, so if you trade channels, you should pay close attention to this aspect.
- The RSI jumps due to changes in prices. The bigger the change in price, the bigger the spike observed in the RSI. Volume has no impact. For RSI calculations, it doesn't matter whether the volume was 1, 100, or 1,00,000. This is why we have to pay attention to the RSI and volume both. The RSI shows the strength of the scrip, and the

volume confirms whether the price movement has good support of the market movers or not.

- You need the data of at least 150 candles for a reliable RSI; otherwise, there will be too many fluctuations, and it won't give reliable signals. So it is not advisable to trade a newly listed stock on the basis of the RSI for 5–6 months if you trade on the basis of daily charts. On the other hand, if you trade on the basis of weekly charts, you will have to wait for 3 years to get those 150 candles. And forget the monthly charts—you won't have that much patience!
- When you train your eyes to recognise patterns like head and shoulders or inverted head and shoulders, you can observe them more frequently on the RSI panel than the price panel. And if you recognise them on the RSI panel, it will certainly improve your odds. You see, your chances of success will improve as the prices don't make a low every month, but the RSI may make a low or high every month due to its limited range of 1 to 100.
- Generally speaking, RSI divergences are very reliable to predict descending channel breakouts, and the results can be very profitable. We should not forget that RSI divergence is a time-tested tool of predicting reversals, and when the trend reverses, it makes strong moves.
- Every stock is unique. It has its unique patterns and signals. This is why we should study the unique behaviour and cues of a stock. For example, one stock might throw hammers at the bottom

frequently; another might give bullish engulfing signals more often. One may give a morning star; another might give a dragonfly doji. For example, Reliance Industries often bounces from the bottom with a morning star or morning doji star. If you know this peculiarity, it will help you when Reliance Industries gives a morning star in a downtrend.

Feedback

Please send your feedback to me at *sdixit123@gmail.com* and leave a suitable rating on Amazon.